GCSE ECONOMICS

Barry Harrison
Charles Smith

COURSEWORK GUIDES

Longman

LONGMAN COURSEWORK GUIDES
Series editors: Geoff Black and Stuart Wall

TITLES AVAILABLE
Art and Design
Biology
Business Studies
CDT: Design and Realisation
Chemistry
Computer Studies
Economics
English
English Literature
Geography
Mathematics
Physics
Religious Studies
Science
Social and Economic History
World History

Longman Group UK Limited,
Longman House, Burnt Mill, Harlow,
Essex CM20 2JE, England
and Associated Companies throughout the world.

© Longman Group UK Limited 1989
All rights reserved; no part of this publication
may be reproduced, stored in a retrieval system,
or transmitted in any form or by any means, electronic,
mechanical, photocopying, recording, or otherwise,
without the prior written permission of the Publishers.

First published 1989

British Library Cataloguing in Publication Data

Harrison, Barry, 1951
   Economics. – (Longman GCSE coursework guides).
   1. England. Secondary schools. Curriculum subjects:
   Economics. G.C.S.E. examinations. Techniques
   I. Title   II. Smith, Charles
   330'.076
   ISBN 0-582-05182-7

Produced by The Pen and Ink Book Company,
Huntingdon, Cambridgeshire

Set in 10/11pt Century Old Style

Printed and bound in Great Britain by
William Clowes Limited, Beccles and London

EDITORS' PREFACE

The introduction of GCSE created many challenges for both teachers and pupils, not least the idea that, for most subjects, the grade awarded should be based not only on examination performance but also on the assessment of certain pieces of coursework. Whilst this concept has been welcomed in most educational circles as relieving some or all of the stress associated with examinations, it is also recognised as imposing other sorts of pressures on pupils. To achieve good results, it is necessary to keep up to date, be organised, and most importantly, maintain an appropriate standard *from the beginning of the course*.

Longman Coursework Guides have been written by experienced examiners to give GCSE candidates help with such tasks as choosing, researching and writing up topics. In addition, the authors give many examples of (and comments upon) typical student assignments.

We believe that the books will stimulate as well as instruct, and will enable students to produce coursework which will truly reflect the level of commitment and effort which the GCSE demands.

Geoff Black and Stuart Wall

AUTHORS' NOTE

Writing coursework can be one of the most enjoyable and rewarding aspects of studying GCSE Economics. However, we think it is impossible to enjoy coursework fully unless you feel you are making progress and are producing work of a standard that fully reflects your ability. We hope that by following the advice in this book you will achieve results in your coursework that both please you and encourage you to continue working for success.

In writing this book we have received a great deal of helpful advice from Mr G.F. Stanlake for which we are very grateful. We have also received a great deal of encouragement from our wives and families and again we acknowledge our gratitude. Last, but not least, we would like to thank the editors of the series, Geoff Black and Stuart Wall, for their advice and guidance.

ACKNOWLEDGEMENTS

The authors are indebted to the following Examination Groups for permission to reproduce syllabus details. Any interpretation of these syllabuses is the responsibility of the authors.

London and East Anglian Group (LEAG)
Midland Examining Group (MEG)
Northern Examining Association (NEA)
Northern Ireland Schools Examination Council (NISEC)
Southern Examining Group (SEG)
Welsh Joint Education Committee (WJEC)

The authors further acknowledge the permission to reproduce material given by the Building Societies Association, the *Glamorgan Gazette*, the *Western Mail*, the *South Wales Echo* and *Parker's Car Price Guide*.

We are grateful to the following students for supplying us with pieces of good coursework from which we have selected examples for use in this book: Matthew Clubb, Jason Davies, Tracy Oglesbee, Gary Owen, Siân Parry, Claire Prime, Ben Thorpe and Carolyn Veck.

Examples of coursework which are not so good were provided by our old friend A. N. Other.

CONTENTS

EDITOR'S PREFACE

AUTHORS' NOTE

ACKNOWLEDGEMENTS

CHAPTER 1	Coursework in Economics	1
	UNIT 1 INTRODUCTION TO COURSEWORK	1
	1.1 Advantages of Coursework	1
	1.2 Types of Coursework in Economics	2
	UNIT 2 SKILLS TO BE TESTED THROUGH COURSEWORK	2
	2.1 Identification, Collection and Use of Information	2
	2.2 Analysis	2
	2.3 Evaluation	4
	2.4 Presentation	5
	UNIT 3 DETAILED MARKING CRITERIA	5
	UNIT 4 COURSEWORK IN EACH EXAMINING GROUP	5
	4.1 Special Schemes	5
	4.2 London and East Anglian Group (LEAG)	6
	4.3 Midland Examining Group (MEG)	7
	4.4 Northern Examining Association (NEA)	7
	4.5 Northern Ireland Schools Examinations Council (NISEC)	8
	4.6 Southern Examining Group (SEG)	9
	4.7 Welsh Joint Education Committee (WJEC)	9
	4.8 International GCSE (IGCSE)	10
	4.9 Syllabuses related to Economics	10
	4.10 Addresses of the Exam Groups	10
CHAPTER 2	Researching a Topic	12
	UNIT 1 CHOOSING A TOPIC AND TITLE	12
	1.1 Choosing a Topic	12
	1.2 Choosing a Title	13
	1.3 Taking Aim	13
	UNIT 2 THE PRESENTATION AND INTERPRETATION OF DATA	14
	UNIT 3 SOURCES OF DATA	15
	3.1 Your own Experiences	15
	3.2 Your Teacher	15
	3.3 The Library	16
	3.4 The Press	16
	3.5 Her Majesty's Stationery Office (HMSO)	17
	3.6 Employment News	18
	3.7 Economic Progress Report	18
	3.8 The Economic Review Data Supplement	18

3.9	TV and Radio	18
3.10	Other Sources	18

UNIT 4 QUESTIONNAIRES 19

4.1	Constructing a Questionnaire	19
4.2	Using a Questionnaire	21

UNIT 5 USING ARITHMETIC AND STATISTICS IN COURSEWORK 22

5.1	Rounding of Figures	22
5.2	Divisions of the Whole	22
5.3	Averages	24
5.4	Diagrams	24

UNIT 6 METHODS OF INVESTIGATION 28

6.1	Formulating a Hypothesis	28
6.2	Testing your Hypothesis	29

UNIT 7 APPLYING ECONOMIC CONCEPTS, THEORIES AND IDEAS 30

7.1	Assignment: Running a family car	30

UNIT 8 SKILLS TO CONCENTRATE ON 31

UNIT 9 PRACTICE QUESTIONS 31

UNIT 10 ANSWERS TO EXERCISES 33

CHAPTER 3 Presenting an Assignment 34

UNIT 1 SALLY'S ASSIGNMENT 34

1.1	Stage 1: Choosing a Topic	34
1.2	Stage 2: Choosing a Title	34
1.3	Stage 3: Taking Aim	34
1.4	Stage 4: Planning	35
1.5	Stage 5: Preparation	35
1.6	Stage 6: Gathering Information	35
1.7	Stage 7: Using Information	35
1.8	Stage 8: Writing and Presentation	35

UNIT 2 EXTRACTS FROM SALLY'S ASSIGNMENT 37

UNIT 3 MATHEW'S ASSIGNMENT 43

UNIT 4 EXTRACTS FROM MATTHEW'S ASSIGNMENT 45

CHAPTER 4 Outline of Marking Schemes 51

UNIT 1 ASSESSMENT CRITERIA 51

UNIT 2 MARKING SCHEMES 52

CHAPTER 5 Assessing your own Coursework 58

UNIT 1 SELF-ASSESSMENT MARK SCHEME 58

UNIT 2 ASSESSMENT OF SALLY AND MATTHEW'S ASSIGNMENT 59

CHAPTER 6 Sample Assignments with Examiner Comments 60

UNIT 1 KEVIN'S ASSIGNMENT: THE PRICE OF SECOND-HAND CARS 60

UNIT 2 KATH'S ASSIGNMENT: LOCATION AND COMPETITION 71

UNIT 3 KIM'S ASSIGNMENT: ADVERTISING 78

UNIT 4 KEN'S ASSIGNMENT: INTERNATIONAL TRADE 80

COURSEWORK IN ECONOMICS

UNIT 1 INTRODUCTION TO COURSEWORK

The widespread introduction of coursework as part of the scheme of assessment is an important feature of GCSE. What coursework actually means, however, is not always clear cut. For Economics, coursework is defined in the GCSE National Criteria as an internally assessed component which must demonstrate the attainment of the *assessment objectives* of the specific syllabus.

The assessment objectives tell you what the examiners are looking for. The five objectives set out below must be assessed in *all* syllabuses in Economics.
Candidates will be expected to:

- demonstrate recall of knowledge in relation to a specified syllabus content.
- demonstrate an ability to use this knowledge in verbal, numerical, diagrammatic, pictorial and graphical form.
- demonstrate an ability to explain and apply appropriate terminology, concepts and elementary theories.
- select, analyse, interpret and apply data.
- distinguish between evidence and opinion, make reasoned judgements and communicate them in an accurate and logical manner.

We look at these assessment objectives in more detail on pages 2–5 below.

To obtain the maximum benefit from coursework it is best to think of it not as something which is *added on*, but rather as something which is part of your *approach to studying that subject*. This is true of *all* coursework, whether it counts directly towards the final grade you are awarded, or whether it is simply a weekly essay submitted to your teacher and returned to you when marked. Think of such work as an opportunity to read more widely, to select and use examples and data to illustrate relevant points of theory, and to develop skills in structuring and presenting information.

1.1 Advantages of coursework

In formal written examinations, candidates are assessed on what they write in answer to different questions within a time limit. Assessment in GCSE Economics is by a combination of written exam and coursework. The minimum amount of marks that can be gained from coursework is 20 per cent of the total. In some cases (see page 6) Examination Groups have opted to make more than 20 per cent of the total marks available for coursework. So what are the advantages that assessment through coursework has over assessment through examination?

- First, assessment through coursework means that a candidate has the opportunity to demonstrate ability and understanding on a *number of occasions* in *different samples of work*. This is likely to increase the reliability of the final grade awarded to a candidate.

- Second, coursework enables teachers to set tasks that are more appropriate to the *individual* student that he or she teaches. Tasks can be set which draw on the particular experience of an individual student, or which involve analysing the economics of those things in which the student has a particular interest. This might be the economics of home or car ownership, or the prospects for a particular local industry. It is thought that such familiarity and interest will help increase student motivation.

▶ Third, assessment through coursework enables candidates to gain credit for demonstrating skills that are important, but which cannot easily be tested by a traditional written examination. For example, candidates can be assessed on their ability:
- to be original in their ideas for the coursework assignment;
- to organise and present an extended piece of work;
- to collect and analyse information and data.

Coursework enables these skills to be tested; in fact it is unlikely that these skills can be tested in any other way.

▶ Fourth, coursework allows students to present work which does *not* have to be completed in a short, pre-ordained period of time. Indeed one of the most common criticisms of formal written examinations is that some candidates find it difficult to work within a time limit. Although the ability to answer questions in a limited amount of time *is* an important skill, other skills can best be tested over an extended piece of work.

1.2 Types of Coursework in Economics

Students often take the term *coursework* to mean the production of a single, detailed assignment or project involving research which can take weeks or even months to complete. As a *general* definition of coursework this is not correct. However, coursework in economics *does* involve the presentation of written work which involves prior research, and it is this type of coursework that we concentrate on in this book. If you would like to know what the coursework requirements are for your Examination Group, and the form that the assignments can take, you will find a detailed discussion of these on pages 5–11.

UNIT 2　SKILLS TO BE TESTED THROUGH COURSEWORK

Different Examination Groups stress different *skills* that are to be assessed by coursework. These skills are known as the assessment objectives. The regulations relating to coursework as specified by each of the Examination Groups are set out on pages 5–11. When preparing assignments for submission it is important that you pay strict attention to the regulations of *your own* Examination Group. Here we consider a breakdown of the skills that coursework will enable you to demonstrate. In other words we examine the skills that are to be tested by coursework. For an indication on the importance of these different skills with respect to your own Examination Group, refer to Chapter 4, pages 51–7.

2.1 Identification, Collection and Use of Information

When considering the suitability of a topic as a basis for coursework it is easy to take for granted the availability of the information required. In fact, *identifying* the kind of information required and then *collecting* it often takes up more time than any other part of research! Before you can decide which information you require and how you are going to collect and use it, you must make a careful plan, or outline, of your project. Only then will you be able to make a proper assessment of what information you require.

It is important that you *only use relevant information* in your project. Remember, marks are awarded for identifying information that is *required* in your project or which can usefully be included in it. No marks will be awarded for the inclusion of irrelevant information. You must therefore think carefully about what information you require and then see if it is available. If it is *not* available, you must then decide what information can be used in its place.

A word of warning is appropriate here and you should pay particular attention to it. Because collecting data can take so much time, it is important to be sure of your needs. If you are not sure, you can waste a great deal of time collecting information which will not be relevant to the investigation you are undertaking. This emphasises the need for careful thought and planning.

2.2 Analysis

For purposes of assessment at GCSE, *analysis* is usually taken to mean the ability to break down information into component parts and to identify the ways in which these parts are related. This sounds quite difficult, partly because it is not always easy to see what the component parts of information are, or how they can be broken down. Let us see what this might mean when applied to Economics.

> **Much analysis is about finding trends and relationships between variables.**

A great deal of analysis in economics is about identifying *trends*, that is the way a variable changes over time. Again, much analysis in economics involves identifying *relationships* between two (or more) variables, for instance between the price of a commodity and the quantity of that commodity demanded by consumers per period of time.

Identifying trends and relationships is very important, because once this has been done we can begin to think about what has *caused* those trends and relationships. Once we know the cause of something it is often easier to find a *cure* for it; this is particularly important where there are undesirable consequences which we would wish to avoid. Also, if we understand the cause of something, it is often possible to use this as a basis for *predicting* what will happen to particular variables in the future.

An example might clarify this point. There is a well established relationship between changes in a country's *money supply* and changes in that country's *rate of inflation*. The faster the money supply rises, the faster the rate of inflation rises. However, identifying that there *is* a general relationship between changes in the money supply and changes in the rate of inflation is just the start. We next have to consider whether changes in the money supply *cause* changes in the rate of inflation, or whether changes in the money supply *follow* changes in the rate of inflation.

Economists have spent many years investigating this issue and still have not reached a firm conclusion. However, it is a very important problem to solve. If it could be proved that the *only cause* of inflation is an increase in the money supply, we would then know how to *cure* inflation. The cure would simply involve a strict control of the money supply. Not only would we know how to cure inflation, we would also be in a position to *predict* what the rate of inflation was likely to be in the future. Suppose we had worked out that a 1% rise in money supply led to a 2% rise in inflation, with a one year time lag. If we knew that money supply had risen by 3% this year, we could then predict a 6% inflation next year.

> **Time lags make it difficult to identify cause and effect. Many variables may change over a period of time.**

Although identifying trends and relationships is very important, it is not always easy. One problem with studying changes in the money supply and changes in the rate of inflation is that a change in the money supply does not lead to an *immediate change* in the rate of inflation. Changes in the rate of inflation only occur after a *time lag*. In other words it might take months, possibly many months, before a change in the money supply has an effect on the rate of inflation. The problem is that while we are waiting to see the effect of a specific change in the money supply, other things can also happen. For example, wages might rise. If prices are eventually seen to rise, how can we know whether the rise in prices was caused by the increase in the money supply rather than by the increase in wages?

Take another example. Consider the effect of a change in the *rate of interest* on the *rate of investment* in the private sector. We might expect to find that an increase in the rate of interest leads to a reduction in the rate of private sector investment, because of the higher cost of borrowing funds for investment. Remember, investment means the creation of man-made aids to production, such as machinery, factory buildings and so on. An increase in the rate of interest increases the *cost* of purchasing additional machinery or factory buildings for most firms, because funds for this purpose are usually borrowed.

Now this is easy to understand; but would we expect to see an increase in the rate of interest one month causing a reduction in the rate of investment in the *same month*? It would be very unusual if we did. Firms make plans about investment which run for quite long periods of time, months or even years in some cases. Because of this, firms do *not* borrow all the funds they require for investment purposes at one go. For example, firms usually purchase additional machinery *in stages*. Once they have started their purchases of additional machinery, an increase in the rate of interest is unlikely to cause them to cancel further purchases that they had already *planned* to make. What is more likely is that some firms will now change their *future plans*. So if there is an increase in the rate of interest one month, we would expect to see investment falling in future months.

However, there are *other factors* that can influence investment by firms. For example, if a firm suddenly started to sell more of its product (in other words, if demand for its product increased) this might persuade the firm to increase investment in plant and machinery. Similarly, a firm might be persuaded to increase investment if a new labour-saving machine was developed. As time passes, all of these factors, and many others, will change. Because of this, it is difficult to see, just by looking at data in the form of tables or graphs, what effect a rise in interest rates alone has had on the level of investment.

> **The rate at which a variable changes is also important.**

Sometimes when we analyse a single variable, such as the rate of inflation or rate of investment, we are interested in whether the variable is rising at a *faster rate* or a *slower rate*. The most common way of doing this is to use percentages. For example, if the rate of inflation in one year is 5 per cent and the following year it is again 5 per cent, this means that prices are rising at a *constant* rate. Each year they are on average 5 per cent higher than the previous year. However, if the following year prices rise by 6 per cent, prices are not only higher, but the *rate at which they are rising* is also increasing. In other words, prices are rising at a faster rate. More is said about how to calculate percentage changes on pages 23–4.

In summary, when analysing data, there are several points to remember:

- Try to identify any *consistency* in the pattern of the data you are using. For example, if you are analysing data from the economy, how often is a change in one variable accompanied by a change in another variable?
- If you have found that two or more variables move together, do not assume that a change in one *causes* a change in the other. This might be the case, but you cannot *assume* that it is. You must consider whether the change in a variable is a 'cause' or an 'effect' of a change in some other variable.
- Remember that *time lags* can affect the relationship between two variables. *Other variables* might also change over a period of time, making it more difficult to identify the true relationship between variables.
- Look out for changes in the *rate* at which a variable is rising or falling.

2.3 Evaluation

Evaluation is not always easy to define, partly because it is very closely related to *analysis*. In GCSE Economics, evaluation usually involves checking that you have *applied* the following skills:

- The ability to use information and analysis to build *arguments* which provide a valid *interpretation of the facts*.
- The ability to use these arguments to reach *conclusions* which are *supported by the facts*.
- Since *information* and *analysis* can often be *interpreted* in different ways, evaluation also involves using *judgement* to decide which argument is more likely to be correct. This will often mean *recognising the assumptions* on which a particular argument is based.
- Evaluation also involves the ability to distinguish between matters of *fact* and matters of *opinion*. Matters of fact can be checked for accuracy. Matters of opinion cannot. We can check the accuracy of a statement such as 'The cost of a new car is £10,000'. However, we cannot check the accuracy of a statement such as 'It is better to buy a new car'. The first is a statement of *fact*, the second is a matter of *opinion*.

> **Analysis will help show us what has happened; evaluation will help explain why it has happened.**

Clearly there are many things to think about. Let us take a more detailed look at some of these points.

To *build* or *develop* an argument is simply another way of saying to put forward a point of view and to support it by facts. Now in a project for GCSE Economics this means *using* the information gathered for your assignment to explain why or how a particular event occurred. For example, you might *collect information* about the prices charged for fresh fruit and vegetables in local shops over a particular period of time, such as a month. You might then *analyse* this data and find that over the month in question many prices of the items you have information on have fallen. You might find that for some items, prices have fallen more than for other items. You are then in a position to *use* your knowledge of economics to explain *why* prices in general have fallen and *why* some prices have fallen more than others. In other words, analysis shows us *what* has happened. Evaluation shows us *why* it has happened. In explaining why prices of fresh fruit and vegetables have fallen you would use your knowledge of *supply and demand*. If you refer to any textbook you use at GCSE, you will see that for most goods and services prices can only fall if there has been either a reduction in demand for that good or service or an increase in supply of that good or service.

One factor that can cause a *reduction in demand* is a reduction in income. However, for this to cause a fall in the price of fresh fruit and vegetables, we have to argue that a reduction in income will cause a general reduction in demand for fresh fruit and vegetables. Even if income for most people in your community has fallen, this is unlikely to cause a reduction in demand for *all* fresh fruit and vegetables. When incomes fall people still have to eat, and there are few substitutes that are cheaper than fresh fruit and vegetables.

Another possibility is that there has been an *increase in supply* of fresh fruit and vegetables. If you have collected information for a month in the summer, this is a very strong possibility. During the summer months weather conditions are usually very favourable, both for growing and picking fresh fruit and vegetables. This is more likely to be the reason for the fall in the prices of fresh fruit and vegetables.

In rejecting the argument that the fall in prices of fresh fruit and vegetables is caused by a reduction in income, you are exercising *judgement*. Similarly, you are exercising judgement in suggesting that it was more likely to have been caused by an increase in supply due to seasonal factors.

Can you see that in providing a *reasoned argument* to explain why prices of fresh fruit and vegetables have fallen, we are drawing on matters of *fact* rather than matters of *opinion*?

2.4 Presentation

How your project is *presented* is very important. Take care to ensure that you present information and argument as clearly as possible. Anyone reading your material should not be confused about:

- your aims
- what the information you include in your assignment shows
- why you have included it
- what your conclusions are
- how you have reached them.

Use this as a checklist when writing your assignment (there is a still more detailed checklist on page 44). Doing this will help to ensure that you are using *all* of the skills necessary to produce an assignment which will earn a high mark.

You can improve the presentation of your work if you pay attention to some elementary points:

- In general do not use abbreviations other than those which are nationally accepted.
- Before submitting your assignment, check it for spelling mistakes and grammatical errors.
- Make sure you check your assignment to ensure that you have given a full account of everything you have considered. You should also make sure that you have included everything in your assignment that you originally planned to include. It is sometimes easy to overlook very important points.

UNIT 3 DETAILED MARKING CRITERIA

Each Examination Group produces guidelines on the amount of credit or number of marks that a candidate can be awarded for displaying the skills discussed above. These guidelines are reproduced in full on pages 52–7. Here we stress that when writing your coursework assignments you should pay particular attention to the marks *your* Examination Group awards for displaying each of these skills. Make sure you have done everything you can to gain maximum marks!

UNIT 4 COURSEWORK IN EACH EXAMINING GROUP

Examination syllabuses provide information on the content of courses, but schools and colleges also receive circulars, memoranda, guidelines, and many other documents relating to all sorts of matters, including coursework assignments. This chapter attempts to draw together all of the information on coursework provided by the Examination Groups.

In compiling this outline we have used the most up-to-date syllabuses and guidelines available. Despite this you should realise that there may be minor changes every year. Your teacher will probably provide you with a recent copy of the relevant syllabus; if not you are strongly advised to obtain one from the Board or Group. Addresses are given on page 11. When writing for a syllabus be sure to ask for any additional information available on economics *coursework*, as this is sometimes issued separately from the actual syllabus.

> **See pages 52–7 for a detailed look at the marking schemes.**

4.1 Special Schemes

The chances are that you will be following 'a mainstream' economics syllabus. However, there are certain *special schemes* available.

MATURE SYLLABUSES

The General Certificate of Secondary Education, as its name implies, is aimed at students in their last year of compulsory secondary education (that is to say, 16-year olds). Some Exam Groups feel that it is desirable to design separate syllabuses for older candidates; others believe that their existing syllabuses are suitable for both 16-year olds and older candidates. Where Examination Boards and Groups offer special 'mature' syllabuses in economics, they all have a coursework requirement.

CHAPTER ONE COURSEWORK IN ECONOMICS

EXTERNAL SYLLABUSES

All Examination Boards and Groups distinguish between full-time and part-time candidates. Certain part-time candidates might be able to enter for a different syllabus to that followed by full-time candidates. This is referred to as an *external* syllabus. Some of these syllabuses do not require coursework. The Boards and Groups refer to part-time candidates as *external candidates* or *private candidates*. If you are a part-time student you should write to your Board or Group for full details of the procedure to follow, and for confirmation that you are classed as an external or private candidate.

It is clear that without the continuous supervision of a teacher, coursework poses a special problem for part-time candidates. However, the Examining Boards and Groups are rapidly moving towards insisting on coursework from *all* candidates: it may soon be impossible to 'escape' from coursework by choosing a special scheme.

Whichever syllabus you follow, you will find that your coursework topics are either *negotiated* or *prescribed* (see Table 1.1). The former are chosen by you with the help and advice of your teacher; the latter are set by the Examining Board or Group.

Table 1.1
Summary of Coursework Requirements; Mainstream Economics Syllabuses

Board/Group	LEAG	MEG	NEA	NISEC	SEG	WJEC
Coursework weighting (per cent)	25	25	30	20	20	20
Number of pieces of coursework	3	3	1, 2 or 3	1	2	1 Field-work, **or** 2 Projects
Approx no. of words per piece of coursework	500 to 1000	Up to 1000	3000, 1500 or 1000	Up to 2000	750 to 1000	2000 (1000 to 3000) **or** 1000 (500 to 1500)
Total no. of words	1500 to 3000	Up to 3000	3000 (Guide line)	Up to 2000	1500 to 2000	2000 (1000 to 3000)
Selection of topics	N	P	N	P	N	N

(N = Negotiated; P = Prescribed)

Here is our interpretation of coursework syllabuses in a form which we hope you will find easy to understand.

4.2 London and East Anglian Group (LEAG)

Coursework accounts for 25 per cent of the total marks for the examination. You will have to submit *three* assignments, each of 500 to 1000 words, with supporting evidence from numerical material, graphs and/or diagrams. The assignments will be on any *three* of the objectives given as headings to each section of the syllabus. These headings are:

1 the fundamental economic problem of scarcity and choice;
2 the operation of the price system in terms of demand and supply;
3 the different forms of enterprise and the reasons for the differences in their scale and organisation in a mixed economy;
4 the location of some major contemporary industries and the reasons for industrial location;
5 the role of financial institutions and their importance for the economy;
6 the structure of, and the reasons for, public revenue and expenditure;
7 the forces, including government, which influence the price level, employment, income, output and economic growth;
8 the importance of internal and international trade, including a knowledge of relevant institutions;

9 the influences at work in the markets for factors of production, including the major institutions in the labour market;
10 the importance of the structure and distribution of population and of changes in these.

Your teacher will give you initial guidance concerning the selection of syllabus areas and content; thereafter you are expected to produce the work without further guidance. The syllabus warns against using a 'scrap-book' approach, and says that graphs and diagrams, when included, should be relevant to the text.

There is a separate syllabus for external candidates, without a coursework requirement. There is also a special scheme for mature students known as the 'Economics 17' syllabus. This is designed for older students who wish to complete the course in one year, and is entirely internally assessed. In this case the whole of the syllabus is assessed as coursework.

Presentation should be in the form of a report rather than an essay, and should include details of the plan adopted, information gathered and discussion/conclusions.

In Option 2 (Economic Principles) the subject area might be economic policy ('Has regional policy in the United Kingdom in the last 20 years been successful?') or industrial matters ('Why have the sales of imported cars reached such a high proportion of the new car market in the United Kingdom?') It is stressed that these sample questions are only examples; it is up to you, under the guidance of your teacher, to 'negotiate' the choice of topic. The Coursework Memorandum suggests that Social Economics provides more scope for fieldwork, whereas Economic Principles is more likely to involve desk research using newspapers, journals, reports and other literature since the topic is more likely to be national or international rather than local.

4.3 Midland Examining Group (MEG)

Coursework carries 25 per cent of the marks for the total examination. You will attempt *three* topics from a list of five provided by the group. Each topic should be not more than 1000 words.

The syllabus states that you must list your sources of published information and (where appropriate) keep a log of visits, surveys and interviews. You are also advised to include photographs, newspaper cuttings, diagrams, maps, graphs, tables, tapes and videos 'where they are relevant to the topic'.

The topics for examination in 1989 are given below. You should obtain the most up-to-date list of topics from your teacher or from the group as soon as possible after starting your course.

1 Using local sources, do a survey on second-hand cars. What factors do advertisers consider important to stress? What factors do you consider determine the prices of second-hand cars?
2 A local study of part of a town, village, or area around the school classifying business functions and types and explaining their presence and importance to the community.
3 A diary following an economic issue, using cuttings and with comments, e.g. a wage claim, or a factory closure.
4 The Local Authority Budget. Briefly consider how the Authority finances and spends its budget and comment on its priorities. Take a sample of people in your neighbourhood (e.g. wage earner, unemployed worker, pensioner) and evaluate the effects of the budget on individuals.
5 Shopping basket survey. Take a sample of ten well-known branded items and cost them in a local small shop, a voluntary retail chain and a national supermarket. Record and comment on the results.

There is no regulation in the syllabus preventing your teacher from giving guidance at any stage of your coursework. You should therefore ask for guidance whenever you feel that you need it.

There is no separate external syllabus, but part-time candidates might be able to take an extra written paper of two hours in place of coursework.

4.4 Northern Examining Association (NEA)

Coursework carries 30 per cent of the total marks for the examination. You can choose either:

    a single assignment which need be no more than 3000 words
or two assignments which need be no more than 1500 words each
or three assignments which need be no more than 1000 words each

The syllabus states that the number of words is given only as a guide, and that as an alternative to written work, equivalent tasks involving the use of oral and/or visual work will be equally acceptable.

Your teacher will be able to advise you on the choice of a topic or topics, and give guidance on how to carry out and present the coursework. Here are some examples of topics provided in the syllabus, for guidance only, to assist candidates and teachers in appreciating the possibilities of coursework:

1 Title: Would unrestricted Sunday trading be beneficial?

   Depending upon the size of the assignment, *practical work* could include surveys of shops, workers, consumers and/or pressure groups to establish local response to Sunday trading.
   Analysis may be concerned with a consideration of the private and social costs and benefits of Sunday trading, from which conclusions may be drawn about the issue. This example gives an opportunity for a group assignment where individual candidates may contribute separately.

2 Title: Why do prices vary between shops?

   A survey of a sample of shops to look at costs and scale of operations and the nature of the local market.
   Analysis would include a comparison of the different types of operation. Conclusions may be drawn as to why consumers are prepared to pay higher prices in some shops. The assignment may concentrate on a particular type of good or service.

3 Title: Local transport – a case for subsidy?

   Recent government policy has drawn attention to the problems of providing transport services in both urban and rural areas. In all areas the cost of providing services exceeds revenue from fares, and subsidies have been introduced.
   Public transport users, car owners and the local commercial community could be interviewed to assess their response to the problem, the implications for them of current policies and possible alternative policies (e.g. privatisation). A group discussion with a representative of the local transport authority could be used to ascertain the rationale behind its policy. A local library search could provide newspaper reports on the issue.
   Analysis would be concerned with revealing the assumptions behind local policy and examining the implications for individuals and groups in the community of using resources to support that policy rather than an alternative one.
   This example provides an opportunity for a group assignment where individual candidates may make separate contributions.

Unlike other boards, the NEA encourages candidates to submit work in 'oral' or 'visual' as well as 'written' form, and it allows candidates to submit assignments as a group. However, teachers are warned that it must be possible to assess the individual candidate's contribution to the work.

The syllabus described above is the 'mainstream' one, known as Syllabus A. There is also a Syllabus B, designed as a 'mature' syllabus, where coursework accounts for 20 per cent of the total marks, as opposed to 30 per cent for Syllabus A. Candidates following Syllabus B write *three* assignments of approximately 500–750 words each from a list of prescribed topics. There is no separate 'external' syllabus. Part-time candidates may sit either Syllabus A or B as appropriate, submitting their coursework directly to their local Board for assessment.

4.5 Northern Ireland Schools Examinations Council (NISEC)

Coursework carries 20 per cent of the total marks for the examination. You will be asked to produce a report (up to a maximum of 2000 words) on a topic set by the Board. Each year the Board produces a list of questions, which will require you to collect, organise, analyse, and present data. You will find guidance on how to do this in Chapter 2. The syllabus states that candidates will be expected to apply their economic knowledge and understanding to the study of economic problems 'within their own economic community'. For the vast majority of NISEC candidates, this means that your coursework will be connected in some way with the economy of Northern Ireland.

The sample topics listed in the syllabus are:

1 Work out the costs and benefits to a young couple of buying, rather than renting, accommodation.
2 What is the occupational structure of employment in your local area? What changes are evident in recent years? Give reasons for and examine the implications of these changes.
3 What economic benefits could be derived from a more intensive use of the facilities of your own school/college?

4 To what extent does the expenditure pattern of senior citizens in your area reflect the national expenditure pattern? Explain and comment on the implications of any significant differences.

Your teacher will give you advice on topic selection; a briefing on recommended source material; and ongoing advice on any problems encountered.

The list of topics provided by the board will alter each year, so it is important that either you or your teacher obtain this list as soon as possible and certainly by the start of the second term of your course. This means that if, for instance, you are sitting the examination in the summer of 1991 you should have seen the list by January 1990 at the latest.

There is a separate external syllabus, with a coursework component, consisting of a report (1000 words maximum) on a topic set by the board. The assignment will then be marked by the board, and followed by an oral examination.

4.6 Southern Examining Group (SEG)

Coursework carries 20 per cent of the total mark for the examination. You will submit *two* items of coursework, each of between 750 and 1000 words.

You will be studying a 'Core' syllabus, together with either Option 1 (Social Economics) or Option 2 (Economic Principles). If you are not sure which option you are following, then ask your teacher to tell you now! The written papers are based mainly on the 'Core' syllabus, while the coursework is based entirely on the 'Option'. You will write *two* pieces of work relating to your chosen syllabus option. (Your coursework must be based on the same option as that chosen for the written examination.)

Your teacher can guide you on the choice of topic, and brief you with advice on source material, textbooks, persons to interview, etc. He or she can also give guidance during the course of your chosen work on any problems encountered, provided that records are kept of all assistance of this type given. Groupwork is acceptable as long as the individual contribution of each candidate can be clearly identified.

The syllabus strongly recommends that all the formally-assessed coursework should be undertaken, completed and marked during the first two terms of the academic year leading up to the examination. However, since it is also suggested that candidates might like to complete more than the required pieces of coursework and select the best two for moderation, there is nothing to prevent you from starting much earlier.

The group publishes a 'Coursework Memorandum' which provides some suggestions for possible areas of study. It regards it as useful to the candidate that '. . . tasks be set in the form of a question to be answered, by means of investigation and data collection, leading to analysis and conclusions'. These issues are discussed in detail in Chapter 2.

For example, an Option 1 (Social Economics) topic might explore the area of local retail and commercial services. Typical questions might be: 'Why has the economic use of land in . . . Street changed in recent years?' or 'Why is the marketing strategy of Shop X different to that of Shop Y?'

4.7 Welsh Joint Education Committee (WJEC)

Coursework carries 20 per cent of the marks for the whole examination. The overall length of the coursework should be approximately 2000 of your own words (with variations allowed between 1000 and 3000 words).

There are two types of coursework assignments:

1 Fieldwork

If you choose this option, then you are asked to apply your economic knowledge and skills to the local economy. Fieldwork involves direct contact within the local community with consumers, producers, and other groups. The assignment should *investigate something specific* within the local economy such as a particular firm or organisation, or *make a comparison between* contrasting units of production in one of the economic 'sectors' (e.g. extractive industry, manufacturing industry, commercial services, or local government). You could, for instance, compare the costs and revenues of a large shop with those of a small shop. The assignment must link with the content of the syllabus by being directly related to topics such as location, wage determination, local authority spending priorities, and so on.

2 Project work

This option enables you to carry out *desk research*, that is, to use *published statistics*, rather than Fieldwork (although there is nothing to stop you carrying out at least part of your research in the locality). If you choose this option you will write two assignments, chosen from the following:

- Simulated Work Experience (for instance, a survey on the activities of the School Bank, or a report on a school minor-enterprise company).
- A Survey of the local or regional market for any agreed product or service using the local press and other information sources, e.g. houses, second-hand cars.
- A Diary following and analysing any relevant economic issue of current interest at local, Welsh, British or international levels, such as trends in local employment opportunities, the rate of inflation, EEC harmonisation policies, development problems in an underdeveloped country.

The WJEC syllabus refers to a *negotiated curriculum,* which means that before you start your coursework you will agree on an outline of your assignment(s) with your teacher. Some guidance on topic selection and choice of title which we hope you will find helpful is given on pages 12–13.

Your teacher can give you guidance and consultation at any stage of your coursework, provided that at the end of the day he or she can be satisfied that your assignments are your own work.

There is no separate external syllabus. Part-time candidates generally sit the mainstream examination which includes coursework. However, private candidates must obtain approval of their coursework proposals directly from the board. They then submit their coursework directly to the board for assessment by a moderator.

4.8 International GCSE (IGCSE)

Non-UK candidates might be interested in the 'International General Certificate of Secondary Education' (IGCSE) syllabuses offered by the University of Cambridge Local Examinations Syndicate (UCLES). The IGCSE Economics syllabus offers a coursework component accounting for either 29 per cent or 25 per cent of the total marks (depending on which combination of written papers is chosen).

Candidates produce *three* pieces of work from a list of topics provided by the Syndicate. Coursework is only available to IGCSE centres approved by the Syndicate. Candidates at other centres take an extra written paper of 1 hour 30 minutes instead of coursework.

4.9 Syllabuses related to Economics

In each of the following three syllabuses, the first piece of coursework is a study of a firm and is a compulsory topic. In the LEAG and SEG schemes, the other pieces are chosen from a list provided by the Group. In the MEG scheme, the first five topics are compulsory, and there is some choice within the sixth.

In each of these three schemes, coursework carries 40 per cent of the total marks for the examination.

Board/Group	Title of Syllabus	Coursework requirement
LEAG	Understanding Industrial Society	3 assignments, no. of words unspecified, marks given for 'quality not quantity'. First assignment worth 20 per cent of exam total, others 10 per cent each.
MEG	Understanding Industrial Society	6 assignments, 1 of 1500 words others of shorter length. First assignment worth 10 per cent of exam total, others worth 6 per cent each.
SEG	British Industrial Society	4 items, each of 700 to 1000 words, all worth equal marks.

4.10 Addresses of the exam groups

Northern Examining Association (NEA)

JMB	Joint Matriculation Board Devas Street, Manchester M15 6EU
ALSEB	Associated Lancashire Schools Examining Board 12 Harter Street, Manchester M1 6HL
NREB	Northern Regional Examinations Board Wheatfield Road, Westerhope, Newcastle upon Tyne NE5 5JZ
NWREB	North-West Regional Examinations Board Orbit House, Albert Street, Eccles, Manchester M30 0WL
YHREB	Yorkshire and Humberside Regional Examinations Board Harrogate Office–31–33 Springfield Avenue, Harrogate HG1 2HW

Sheffield Office–Scarsdale House, 136 Derbyshire Lane, Sheffield S8 8SE

Midland Examining Group (MEG)

Cambridge	University of Cambridge Local Examinations Syndicate Syndicate Buildings, 1 Hills Road, Cambridge CB1 2EU
O & C	Oxford and Cambridge Schools Examinations Board 10 Trumpington Street, Cambridge; and Elsefield Way, Oxford
SUJB	Souther Universitities' Joint Board for School Examinations Cotham Road, Bristol BS6 6DD
WMEB	West Midlands Examinations Board Norfolk House, Smallbrook Queensway, Birmingham B5 4NJ
EMREB	East Midlands Regional Examinations Board Robins Wood House, Robins Wood Road, Aspley, Nottingham NG8 3NH

London and East Anglian Group (LEAG)

London	University of London Schools Examinations Board Stewart House, 32 Russell Square, London WC1B 5DN
LREB	London Regional Examinations Board Lyon House, 104 Wandsworth High Street, London SW18 4LF
EAEB	East Anglian Examinations Board The Lindens, Lexden Road, Colchester, Essex CO3 3RL

Southern Examining Group (SEG)

AEB	The Associated Examining Board Stag Hill House, Guildford, Surrey, GU2 5XJ
Oxford	Oxford Delegacy of Local Examinations Ewert Place, Summertown, Oxford OX2 7BZ
SREB	Southern Regional Examinations Board Avondale House, 33 Carlton Crescent, Southampton, SO9 4YL
SEREB	South-East Regional Examinations Board Beloe House, 2–10 Mount Ephraim Road, Tunbridge TN1 1EU
SWEB	South-Western Examinations Board 23–29 Marsh Street, Bristol, BS1 4BP

Wales

WJEC	Welsh Joint Education Committee 245 Western Avenue, Cardiff CF5 2YX

Northern Ireland

NISEC	Northern Ireland Schools Examinations Council Beechill House, 42 Beechill Road, Belfast BT8 4RS

Cambridge

IGCSE	International General Certificate of Secondary Education 1 Hills Road, Cambridge CB1 2EU

RESEARCHING A TOPIC

UNIT 1 — CHOOSING A TOPIC AND TITLE

Before you begin your coursework, there are three things that you must do:

- Choose a topic;
- Choose a title;
- Take aim.

Let us look at each of these in some detail.

1.1 Choosing a Topic

Some Examining Groups and Boards have 'prescribed' topics; others have topics which are 'negotiated'. What do these terms mean? Further details are given on pages 5–11 in this book, but in a nutshell, *prescribed topics* are given by the Examining Board, usually in a list of about half-a-dozen. Students select a topic from this list. In a class of students following prescribed topics, large numbers of candidates are likely to submit pieces of coursework on very similar themes. *Negotiated topics* on the other hand, are chosen by the candidate and teacher between them; there is therefore no reason why any two members of a class should choose the same topic. They might all be different.

Whether topics are prescribed or negotiated, it is important to consult your teacher *before* making a choice. Tell your teacher which topic interests you, why it interests you, how you intend to approach the topic and so on.

It is essential to choose an area of the syllabus which is 'right' for you. Look for something which you find interesting, and where it will be relatively easy for you to collect information. It is a very good idea to include some research from the area in which you live. Teachers and examiners like to see economic theory being related to your immediate environment. Local fieldwork can be very rewarding, especially since you can then find out how economics is related to your own environment. Research which relies too much on books is unlikely to help you do this.

> **involving the local community**

Fieldwork involves gathering information that is not always readily available in the classroom or in the textbooks you will use on your course. Instead you must gather information from the community in which you live. This means that if you live in Britain, you cannot carry out fieldwork on the economy of France. It is not local and you would have difficulty in popping across the Channel during an economics lesson! However, you might find that a local firm makes use of components transported from a factory in Rouen, or that the grapes in your local supermarket are imported from Bordeaux. This gives you an opportunity to study a topic such as international trade from a *local* point of view.

> **In fieldwork you collect your own information and data.**

Suppose you decide to carry out an assignment which involves 'desk research', that is, using material which has already been published such as government statistics, rather than fieldwork. If you do, remember that there is usually some *local viewpoint* to an economic topic which will enable you to carry out *at least part* of your research in the locality. For example, by 1992 all barriers to international trade within the EEC are to be removed. You might investigate the likely effects of this on particular aspects of the community in which you live.

> **Desk research involves published material.**

Try to choose a topic which is *not too broad*, but which concentrates on a *specific issue* or *problem*. Look for a *theme* which is not too run-of-the-mill, but gives you something of a challenge and the chance to be original. Examiners like to see assignments where the candidate has shown some 'flair'. Don't be afraid of being ambitious, but at the same time be realistic. You need a topic which you can cope with using the knowledge and methods of

CHAPTER TWO CHOOSING A TOPIC AND TITLE

GCSE Economics. You are not (yet) an 'A' level candidate or a Ph.D. student!

Many candidates are tempted to choose topics which are too historical, or too geographical, or which would be better suited to a project for Commerce or Business Studies. Of course these subjects are related to Economics, but you should always remember that Economics is a distinct subject in its own right.

> **Make sure the topic is relevant to Economics.**

What is it that distinguishes an economic topic from one belonging to any other discipline? Economics is about *making the best use of scarce resources*. It should therefore be possible to relate your topic somehow to the fundamental economic problems of *what?*, *how?* and *for whom?* Should you have any doubt about the meaning of ideas such as these, then re-read the first couple of chapters of your Economics textbook. If you can convince yourself and your teacher that these links can be made, then your topic *is* an economic one.

One of the most exciting things about coursework assignments is the fact that because *you* do the work, you can turn up discoveries which you never expected. We hope this is true of your assignments, but even if it isn't we hope you find coursework assignments interesting, informative and enjoyable.

1.2 Choosing a Title

Choosing a *title* for your assignment is not always easy. However, it is very important and it is something you should think carefully about.

The title you choose should give a clear indication of what your coursework assignment is going to be about, and what its contents are likely to be. Avoid vague titles or titles which are not *specifically* related to the topic you are investigating. For example, if you are investigating the effect of a pit closure on the local community, avoid a title such as: 'An Investigation into the Coal Industry'. Choose instead: 'The Effect of the Closure of Colliery X on the Town of X'. Even this might be too broad for the topic you wish to concentrate on and might be narrowed down to something like: 'The Effect of the Closure of Colliery X on House Prices in the Town of X'. Similarly, avoid a title such as: 'The British Steel Industry'. Choose instead: 'The Factors Determining the Location of the Abbey Steel Works in Port Talbot'.

> **Make your title specific rather than general.**

In a nutshell, the title of your coursework assignment should accurately reflect the *contents* of the material you intend to submit. It should not be a detailed summary of your assignment, but should give an indication of the ground covered. Some titles from assignments referred to in this book will show you what we mean:

- 'An Investigation into the Costs of Running a Family Car'
- 'The Factors that Determine Demand for a Car'
- 'How and Why do the Advertising Activities of Large Firms Differ from the Advertising Activities of Small Firms?'

We think you will agree that these titles give an initial guide to the expected contents of the assignment. They do not tell you exactly what material you will find in an assignment or what the conclusion will be; but they do give an idea.

One thing to remember is that when you have completed an assignment, the final outcome is sometimes different from what was originally planned. If this happens, you must consider altering the title of your assignment.

1.3 Taking Aim

Starting an assignment without having any *aims* is like catching a bus without knowing where it is going, or firing a rifle which has no sights and no target.

Having selected a title you must concentrate your mind on some *specific tasks*. Without something specific in mind your project will be aimless and rambling. You need a *target*, so that you can take aim carefully, and keep it in your sights while you fire away with your coursework assignment.

A good plan is to make a *hypothesis* (or theory). Unfortunately, in Britain, the term hypothesis is thought of as rather a clever word, which only very brainy people would ever use. This is not so in other countries. For instance, in ordinary everyday conversation, a Spaniard might say, quite naturally, 'Hay mucha nube y tengo una hypotesis que va a llover' – there's a lot of cloud and I've a hypothesis that it's going to rain.

> **Try to develop a hypothesis that can be tested.**

A hypothesis is simply a theory which can be *tested*. It is a sensible assumption, or a reasonable guess. The hypothesis can be put forward as a simple statement which the *evidence* that you collect will either support or contradict. For example:

'Large shops have lower costs than small shops'.

This is a statement which might be supported or contradicted by evidence. It does not really matter whether the hypothesis is right or wrong, as long as it can be *tested*. A well thought-out hypothesis will give you an aim and a sense of direction.

Another way of stating your aims is to ask a *question*. This is not terribly different from making a hypothesis. For instance:

'What advantages do large shops have over small shops?'

This is a question, but its aim is similar to that of the hypothesis stated above; an assignment aimed at *answering* this question would probably not turn out very differently from an assignment aimed at testing the hypothesis.

In thinking of a hypothesis or in posing a question you will be looking for ways of relating your knowledge of economic facts and theories to the world about you: in other words, of making your economic textbooks and course notes 'come alive'. If you *can* do this, you are well on the way to writing a successful coursework assignment. Much more is written about how to form and test a hypothesis on pages 28–9.

UNIT 2 — PRESENTATION AND INTERPRETATION OF DATA

The use of *data* in coursework assignments is very important, particularly if you are to obtain a high mark. Data can mean any kind of material which is used to support or reject an argument, or to illustrate or clarify a particular idea. This definition of data is very broad and could include a great many things such as photographs, cuttings from the press, diagrams, statistical tables, interviews with local people, and so on.

❝ Use data where it is relevant to your argument. ❞

Whatever *type* of data you include in your assignment, it is very important to use it in the *appropriate context*. Too often students include data in their assignments without really explaining *why* it has been included. There is probably only one thing worse than this, and that is not to include data at all! It is therefore vitally important that you:

1 Consider the *reasons* for including particular data in your assignment.
2 Explain the *relevance* of the data, that is explain what the data shows, in the body of your assignment.

Chapter 6 provides some examples of assignments. When reading these, try and look at the variety of ways in which data has been used and how the reasons for using that data have been explained.

The *National Criteria for Economics* are guidelines which all boards and groups must follow when designing their syllabuses. These indicate that, among other things, one of the general aims of the GCSE Economics course is:

'To develop the ability to use language and numbers effectively and to develop diagrammatic and graphical applications to assist in the communication of ideas'.

Coursework assignments provide an ideal opportunity to achieve these aims and, when preparing assignments, it would be useful to remember this.

However, a timely word of warning is given here. You must take great care to ensure that you present data in a way that is *relevant* to the topic you are writing about. The following quotation from a chief examiner in GCSE Economics stresses this point:

The fact that marks can be earned for 'presentation' has also created its problems. Candidates have spent hours producing attractive bar charts or pie charts. It has been a labour of love but often little to do with Economics. Sadly, pages of diagrams were allowed to pass without comment and effort here seemed to have been diverted away from the more difficult skills of analysis and evaluation. My own students attempted an investigation of the demand for local video hire shops. In the event they could only interview a very small number of customers. The information produced could be tabulated and presented diagrammatically but of much greater interest was the question of reliability of the results and what they told about the nature of demand in this market.

The warning is clear. Presenting data, and the form in which you present it, are important. However, presenting assignments is not simply a matter of presenting data. It is a matter of *exploring* important issues and using data to *illustrate* and *support* an argument which is part of the overall investigation.

> UNIT 3 SOURCES OF DATA

For any assignment you prepare, the type of data you require will partly depend on the topic you are investigating. Some will be readily available from within your own household. For example, you might undertake an investigation into the cost of running the household motor car or domestic freezer. On the other hand, if you are investigating the changing nature of Britain's overseas trade, the information you require is unlikely to be available from within your own household. Whatever your assignment we hope you will find the data you need from the sources given here.

3.1 Your own Experiences

Economics is a subject which lends itself easily to the preparation of coursework. It is sometimes said that in Economics there are many questions for which we have no ready answers. This is because Economics deals with *real world* problems and these are constantly changing. You are probably already familiar with some of the problems Economics attempts to deal with. If you live in an area such as Scotland or the North East where *unemployment* is traditionally well above the national average, or if you have the unfortunate experience of having someone in your own household unemployed, you will already have first-hand experience of at least one economic problem! Another economic problem that you are probably even more familiar with is *inflation*. This is generally taken to mean a situation that exists when the prices of most goods and services that we buy are rising.

Your own experience of economic events, such as unemployment in your neighbourhood or changes in the prices of goods and services your household purchases, can provide a valuable source of data for use in your assignment. For example, one idea might be to conduct a study of how accurately changes in the rate of inflation, as reported by the statisticians, actually reflects the experiences of *people you know*. They are unlikely to be affected equally, since people in different age groups consume different goods and services and the prices of these do not always change by the same amount. For example, the Retail Price Index, which is used to measure the overall rate of inflation, might rise over a particular period by 5 per cent. However, the prices of goods and services which older people tend to buy, such as warm clothing, heating, food and so on, might rise by *more than* 5 per cent over the same period.

Personal studies of this nature can be very interesting and they enable you to learn a great deal about *economics in action*, that is about the way in which some of the things you read about in your textbook operate in practice! However, one possible problem with this kind of assignment is that the data on which your assignment is based is likely to change quite *slowly over time*. For example, unemployment or the prices of goods and services in your neighbourhood are unlikely to change much from one week to the next. Such data is therefore unlikely to be suitable as the basis for many assignments. Nevertheless, it might still be possible to include this type of data as *part* of your assignment.

Personal experience is involved throughout economics in a *variety* of ways. For instance, we make *economic choices* every day of our lives; deciding what we shall spend our money on involves an economic choice. So does deciding how we will allocate our time between the different things we wish to do, and so on. One way in which personal experiences might form the basis of an assignment is examined on pages 30–31 when we consider the cost of running the family motor car in some detail.

3.2 Your Teacher

Do not neglect the value of your *teacher* as a source of data. Indeed, depending on the data you require, your teacher might well prove to be the most comprehensive and reliable source of information you have access to! All teachers of Economics gather a large amount of facts and figures over time. Much of this is used by them when teaching different parts of the Economics course. However, your own teacher might not have used a particular set of data that you require at the time you are writing up your assignment. Whatever the case, if you require a *particular type of data* your teacher might be able to supply you direct or, if not, to guide you to an appropriate source from which you can obtain the information you require. In particular, many schools and colleges are now equipped with computer facilities which you might be able to use to obtain information stored on disc. In some cases you might even be able to use a networked database such as TTNS, Prestel or some other viewdata system.

Not only is your teacher likely to be extremely helpful in providing data, he or she will be able to offer advice if you are having difficulty *interpreting the data* you have obtained. Interpreting data can sometimes be very difficult because it does not always follow the pattern you expect from reading your textbooks. Much of the data in textbooks is *hypothetical*, in other words *invented data* which has been carefully selected to illustrate a particular point. When you collect your *own* data, especially facts and figures, it will not always be as easy to understand as the data you see in textbooks.

There is nothing wrong in seeking advice about what the information you have gathered shows and your teacher will no doubt be happy to help. However, you must remember that coursework is supposed to be something you write yourself and therefore your teacher is not able to tell you what to write.

3.3 The Library

Again a very useful source of data is the *library*. Your school or college library will have books to which you should refer for information on whatever topic you are researching before preparing your assignment. The main source of data in the library is likely to be books which either deal specifically with the topic you are investigating or which contain chapters which deal with it. Similarly, your local public library will have books that might be useful in preparing assignments.

We are not suggesting that you read every book which deals with the topic you are investigating, but we do feel that it is very important to read more than just one book. This will enable you to *compare* what one person has written about a particular topic with what another person has written. Reading *different* viewpoints may help improve your understanding; it may also help you to form your *own* opinions, enabling you to decide how much of what each person has written you agree with or disagree with. It will also enable you to give a more *balanced* discussion of both sides of an argument, instead of simply presenting one side.

Public libraries in particular will often have many other sources of information that might be important when preparing assignments. Many of the publications listed below, such as newspapers, will be readily available. However public libraries also have *trained staff* who will often be able to give advice on whether particular facts and figures are available, where they can be found and what other data might also be useful in the particular investigation you are carrying out. In particular, the *reference section* of most modern town or city libraries will have many journals and government publications. If you politely ask the reference librarian for assistance, he or she will usually be only too pleased to help. However, do try to be *specific* in your request for help.

3.4 The Press

Newspapers provide an extremely useful source of information. They provide up-to-date *commentary* on national economic issues such as changes in the rate of inflation. In addition, *local papers* provide information on matters closer to home and these will often be of more use when preparing an assignment. Here again, consulting *different* newspapers can help provide a clearer understanding of the issues and can help you form your own ideas. Often newspaper articles contain facts and figures in the form of numerical tables as well as charts and graphs. Most public libraries stock a range of newspapers and a great deal of information can be obtained by checking back issues. To check through several newspapers over a number of weeks is, of course, a time-consuming process. However, several topics are reported at *specific dates*, such as a particular day of the month, and if you find out what these dates are, you can considerably reduce the time you spend searching. For example, changes in the level of *unemployment* nationally and in the different regions, as well as changes in the *rate of inflation* as measured by changes in the retail price index, are regularly monitored and are reported *monthly* on the television news and in the press. The same is true of the current account of the *balance of payments* which gives details of how much we spend on goods and services from abroad (imports) and how much we earn by selling goods and services abroad (exports).

Other economic events are sometimes reported even more frequently. For example, changes in the *rate of exchange* between sterling and the dollar, or changes in the *average price of shares* in joint-stock companies are sometimes reported *daily*! On the other hand, the privatisation of a particular industry such as the gas industry is reported in the run-up to privatisation and at the time privatisation happens, but rarely thereafter. Similarly, reports by the Monopolies and Mergers Commission on whether a particular merger or take-over bid by one company for another is likely to be beneficial to the economy or not, are reported at the time they occur; but afterwards they cease to be topical and are no longer of current interest to the majority of people.

No guidance can be given on when to check the newspapers for such occasional information unless you or your teacher can remember that the topic you are researching was reported at a particular time. Despite this the press and news reports can be a major source of data for inclusion in assignments. Some newspapers are more likely to be helpful than others. If you are thinking of looking at newspapers as a source of information, ask your teacher for advice on which ones he or she thinks it is best to consult.

One useful way of checking articles on a *specific topic* is to use *The Times Index* which may be in the local library. This is a monthly index, by subject heading and by author, to the pages of *The Times* newspaper. These pages may then be available in the library, perhaps on microfilm. Consult the librarian.

3.5 Her Majesty's Stationery Office (HMSO)

For most statistical information HMSO is probably the most thorough and comprehensive source available. Several HMSO publications are readily available in public libraries, but here again some might be available in your own school or college library. Two publications that are almost certain to be available in most public libraries are *The Annual Abstract of Statistics* and *Social Trends*. A summary of the contents of these publications is given in Tables 2.1 and 2.2.

Table 2.1 HMSO Publications; Annual Abstract of Statistics.

Population (Age and Sex Structure, Regional Distribution etc)
Employment (Different Industries, Unemployment, Earnings, Trade Unions etc)
Production (Different Industries)
External Trade (Value of Exports and Imports)
Balance of Payments
National Income and Expenditure
Personal Income, Expenditure and Wealth
Home Finance (Central Government and Local Government)
Banking and Other Financial Institutions (Money Supply, Interest Rates, etc)
Prices

Table 2.2 HMSO Publications; Social Trends.

Population
Employment (Including Special Employment Measures)
Income and Wealth
Resources and Expenditure (National Income, Prices, Central and Local Government Expenditure etc)

For many of the entries listed in the contents, both publications give information going back several years so it is easy to see how the different aggregates have *changed over time*. For example, look at the annual rates of unemployment or the numbers in the working population and you will see what we mean. A further point to remember is that the *Annual Abstract of Statistics* presents data entirely in the form of tables, whereas *Social Trends* gives some data in the form of charts and other data in the form of statistical tables.

There are many other publications produced by HMSO which might be even more use to you than the two mentioned above. Unfortunately they are unlikely to be so readily available. Nevertheless, it might be worth finding out exactly which HMSO publications your local library has available.

A publication by the Central Statistical Office (CSO) that is particularly useful to Economists is 'Economic Trends' which is published monthly and so gives recent figures for the aggregates covered. The contents of Economic Trends are given in Table 2.3.

Table 2.3 Economic Trends

Expenditure on GDP
Personal Disposable Income and Consumption
Retail Sales
Gross Domestic Product and Shares of Income and Expenditure
Output Per Person Employed
National Employment and Unemployment
Regional Unemployment Rates
Average Earnings
Prices
Visible Trade
Balance of Payments Current Account
Exchange Rates
Money Supply
General Government Receipts and Expenditure
Interest Rates, Security Prices and Yields

3.6 Employment News

This is a monthly publication which is distributed free of charge by the Department of Employment to schools and colleges. Each issue contains articles about developments in the labour market, such as changes in the government's training initiatives. It also gives monthly data going back several months on the rate of inflation, as measured by the Retail Price Index, and on the level of unemployment.

3.7 Economic Progress Report

This publication is also distributed free of charge to schools and colleges. It is published five times a year and contains articles on the performance of the UK economy in general. It also contains articles on specific aspects of the economy, such as changes in the amount and type of savings in the UK, changes in investment in the UK, what the single European Market will mean for the UK, and so on.

You might find some of these articles a little difficult to understand. However, a feature of most articles is that they contain *data* which might very well be useful in the preparation of coursework. Some of the facts and figures given, as well as the charts and graphs, might be especially useful. The Economic Progress Report has another feature that might be useful in the preparation of assignments. On the back page of each issue there are a series of graphs showing how some important statistics, such as unemployment and the rate of inflation, have changed over time. If they are relevant to your investigation these diagrams could easily be incorporated into your assignment either in support of an argument you are dealing with, or as something which you might wish to explain. Information about this publication can be obtained from:

Economic Progress Report
Publications Division
Central Office of Information
Hercules Road
London SE1 7DU

3.8 The Economic Review Data Supplement

The Economic Review Data Supplement is an annual publication which is really aimed at students on 'A' level and degree courses. It contains facts and figures often going back several years. Your teacher might have a copy of this in the library and, if it is useful, he or she might lend it to you for your assignment.

3.9 TV and Radio

There are a number of TV and radio programmes which you might find useful including 'Money Box' (Radio 4), 'The Money Programme' (BBC 2), and 'The Business Programme' (Channel 4). You should also keep an eye open for one-off documentaries and current affairs items which might be relevant. Sit by the set with a note-book if you are unable to record a programme and try to jot down a summary of the main points which you might wish to include in your assignment. Remember, discussion programmes are useful because you hear both sides of an argument.

3.10 Other Sources

A variety of other sources may provide useful information, data and ideas, depending of course on the topic and title you have chosen.

BANK REVIEWS

Often available free, on application.
Barclays Review, published quarterly, Group Economics Department, 54 Lombard Street, London EC3P 3AH.
Lloyds Bank Review, published quarterly, The Editor, Lloyds Bank Review, 71 Lombard Street, London EC3P 3BS.
Midland Bank Review, published quarterly, The Manager, Public Relations Department, Midland Bank p.l.c., PO Box 2, Griffin House, Silver Street Head, Sheffield S1 3GG.

National Westminster Bank Quarterly Review, published quarterly, The Editor, National Westminster Bank p.l.c., 41 Lothbury, London EC2P 2BP.
The Three Banks Review, published quarterly, The Royal Bank of Scotland p.l.c., Edinburgh EH2 ODG.

BRITISH ECONOMY SURVEY

Published by Longman, Longman House, Burnt Mill, Harlow, Essex CM20 2JE.
A useful, twice-yearly, update on the current state of the British economy. Eight main sections: Industrial Structure; Public Sector; Monetary System; Public Finance; Industrial Relations and Employment; Balance of Payments; World Economy; and Housing. Published in October and April.

LLOYDS BANK ECONOMIC BULLETIN

Published by Group Economics Dept, Lloyds Bank, 71 Lombard St, London EC3P 3BS.
Monthly, on request. Each issue covers a topic of current interest, presenting economic principles in a manner understandable to non-economists. Also included is a section on changes in the main economic indicators.

UNITED KINGDOM IN FIGURES

Published by the Central Statistical Office, Press and Information Service, Great George Street, London SW1P 3AQ.
This pocket-sized abstract provides current facts and figures on population, employment, the environment, the standard of living and the National Accounts. Free from the above address.

UNIT 4 QUESTIONNAIRES

> A questionnaire can be an important means of gathering information.

One of the most popular ways of obtaining information is to carry out a survey of public opinion using a *questionnaire*. A questionnaire simply consists of a list of questions which individuals, who it is hoped will participate in the survey, are invited to answer. The construction and use of a questionnaire can therefore form an important part of the process of research.

The success of any survey involving the use of a questionnaire depends on many factors. There is no doubt that one which is particularly important is the way in which questions are worded. The following section outlines some important points to remember when constructing and using questionnaires.

4.1 Constructing a Questionnaire

The starting point when constructing a questionnaire, is to consider *exactly* what information you require. If you are at all unclear about the specific information you require, and the part this information will play in your assignment, you will waste your time drawing up and using a questionnaire. In these circumstances the results of your survey are unlikely to provide you with the material you require because you are unlikely to have asked the appropriate questions in the first place! For example, if the broad topic you are investigating is *advertising*, you must ask yourself, and answer, questions such as these:

▶ Do you wish to focus on advertising generally or do you wish to be more specific and focus on a particular aspect of advertising?
▶ Do you want to compare the way large firms advertise their products with the way small firms advertise their products?
▶ Do you want to research the reaction of consumers to different forms of advertising, trying to discover which they think are most effective and why.
▶ Do you want to investigate the effect of television advertising on what older people buy compared with what younger people buy?

> asking the right questions

Only by *clearly identifying* the type of information you require at the very outset will you be able to pose the *types of questions* that will provide you with this information.

Having decided *what* you are going to do and the *information you require* you are now in a position to begin constructing your questionnaire. What are the major aspects you should consider when *phrasing your questions*?

- First, questions should be easy to understand and be as brief as possible. If a question is difficult to understand because it contains words that people are unfamiliar with, or because it is so long that people are unclear what they are being asked, the answers given are likely to be vague. A good question is *brief, clear* and *straight to the point*.
- Second, the answers that the *respondents* (people who are answering your questions) are expected to give should be as brief as possible. Since you will have to write down the answers you must remember that people are more likely to give you their time if you only detain them a short while, than if you attempt to detain them for a considerable period! Imagine the response you would receive if you asked a question such as: 'What do you think of advertising?' The question is certainly brief, but it is so *general* that it is almost meaningless. The first thing people would wish to know is what *specific* type of advertising you are referring to!
- In addition to being brief, clear and direct, questions should as far as possible follow a *logical sequence*, so that respondents do not feel they are 'back-tracking'! It is very off-putting for people to think they are being asked a question which they feel they have already answered. Remember, many of the people you ask to interview might be in a hurry. In any case nobody likes to think their time is being wasted.
- Take care how you *phrase* questions so that people know exactly what they are being asked. For example, if you are asked the question, 'Do you think television advertising is beneficial?', the answer depends on how you *interpret* the word 'beneficial'. Someone who works for independent television might be inclined to answer 'yes' because it clearly benefits them. Without income from advertising they might not have a job! Similarly, someone who works for a firm whose products are regularly advertised on television might be inclined to answer 'yes', since they are likely to feel that they benefit from it. However, someone else might argue that television advertising is not beneficial if it encourages people to consume products which are harmful to them. So try to avoid questions which use 'ambiguous phrases', i.e. words which can be interpreted in different ways.
- In general, avoid asking *personal* questions. In particular never ask people what they earn. This is guaranteed to cause offence. If you really need this kind of information ask a person's occupation and how long they have worked at it. Your careers teacher or economics teacher should then be able to help you *estimate* their earnings. Be *very* tactful when asking people their age. Ask if they are under 21, or over 21, retired and so on. Young people and older people are usually happy to give their age. It's the ones in the middle who cause problems!

> **Points to bear in mind when developing you questionnaire.**

If you have filled in a questionnaire yourself you will probably be aware that there are several different types of question used. However, the most commonly used questions are:

1 Dichotomous questions.
2 Open-ended questions.

DICHOTOMOUS QUESTIONS

These are straightforward questions which can usually be answered by a simple 'yes' or 'no'. For example, in terms of investigating the impact of advertising on consumer purchases you might begin with a question such as: 'Do you have a television set?'; or 'Did you watch television yesterday evening between 8 o'clock and 10 o'clock?' (Notice the wording of the second question. Why would it be inappropriate to simply ask, 'Did you watch television yesterday between 8 o'clock and 10 o'clock?')

> **questions with a simple yes/no answer**

OPEN-ENDED QUESTIONS

These questions give much more scope for respondents to express their own opinions. Questions such as 'Do you think the advertising of alcohol on television should be restricted to certain hours only?'; or 'Do you think there is excessive advertising of alcohol on television?' In both cases the respondent is asked for an *opinion*, but it is hoped that in neither case will the answer be excessively long.

Using open-ended questions might mean that you will use your questionnaire as a 'prompt' and conduct a face-to-face 'interview' or 'question-and-answer' session. This type of questioning can be very rewarding, provided that you have a clear idea of what you want to ask before you start your interview. Sometimes you can make up additional questions as you go along and explore ideas which you might not have considered before the interview. If the respondent is willing, a tape-recorder is a useful accessory to interviews of this sort.

> **questions with longer answers**

4.2 Using a Questionnaire

Before *using* any questionnaire you are strongly advised to read the following warning:

> **WARNING**
>
> Where an assignment involves the use of questionnaires, **do not** interview strangers in their own homes or put yourself in any other hazardous situation. If you interview strangers, you should do this in public places, preferably with other friends present. If you wish to interview business people on their business premises you should always make an appointment first. Ask a friend to accompany you. In a nutshell, if you conduct interviews by yourself, restrict these to family and friends.

Choosing people to answer

Having constructed a questionnaire you must also remember that there are problems to avoid when using it. In the first place you must decide *who* you are going to select to answer your questions. In some cases you might require a purely *random sample* of people, but in others you might wish to concentrate on a *particular group* of people. For example, are you interested in the impact of television advertising on men and women or are you more interested in the impact of television advertising on women only? Are you interested in demand for a product from all age groups, or from teenagers only?

> **Include the right people.**

Your behaviour

You must also remember to be *polite* and *attentive*. Remember, when you stop people and ask them to take part in your survey they might be in a hurry. They are more likely to assist you if you are courteous and explain that the information you require is for use in an assignment you are writing as a part of your GCSE Economics course. If you explain this, people are more likely to co-operate. After all, many of them might also have children doing GCSEs! You will also find people more co-operative if you are attentive to their answers. Do not allow yourself to be unduly distracted by what is going on around you. Look at the people to whom you are addressing your questions. When they have answered all of your questions don't forget to thank them and so on.

'Leading' your answers

Another problem to avoid is that of '*leading*' the respondent into giving a particular answer. In other words, you must take care when asking your questions not to give the impression that you require a particular answer or that one answer is preferable to another. You can easily give this impression if you emphasise one response in preference to another, for example by rushing past some responses but taking your time with others, or by altering the tone of your voice when referring to a particular alternative. When asking your questions make sure that nothing in your voice or the expression on your face gives any clue to the particular answer you would find most useful.

When writing up your assignment remember to include a *copy* of your questionnaire. If it is appropriate you might include a discussion of the *reasons* you asked particular questions. It will of course be necessary to include an *analysis* of the *responses* you received to the different questions. In other words, what does your survey suggest about the impact of television advertising on what your different groups of people buy.

To do this it will first be necessary to add together all of the responses you received to each of your questions. Next it will probably be necessary to use percentages to show what *proportion* or percentage of the people you interviewed gave a particular answer to a question. You might then use the results you obtain from calculating percentages to support your arguments or your conclusions. An example to illustrate these points is shown here:

Question No	No of people who answered				Percentage who answered			
	a)	b)	c)	d)	a)	b)	c)	d)
1	6	4	NA	NA	60	40	NA	NA
2	9	1	NA	NA	90	10	NA	NA
3	2	3	0	5	20	30	0	50

NA = Not Applicable. (This might be because questions 1 and 2 required only "Yes" or "No" as an answer.)

If you are unsure how to calculate percentages don't worry. These are explained with examples on pages 23–4 and some practice questions, with answers, are given on pages 31–2.

UNIT 5 USING ARITHMETIC AND STATISTICS IN COURSEWORK

> **Simple numerical techniques can much improve your coursework analysis.**

You might be tempted to read this section later when you come to *use* the techniques it deals with in *writing your assignment*. However, we think it might be better to read it now and to master the techniques it covers so that you can decide which of them will be most useful to you when you are *analysing your data*.

Economics deals with the real world. It attempts to explain such questions as what causes inflation, or why consumers buy more of a good when its price falls. To help find answers to these questions economists use a variety of *arithmetical and statistical techniques*. An understanding of some of the elementary techniques used by economists, is necessary at GCSE level. However, a surprising number of Economics' students find these simple arithmetical and statistical techniques off-putting. Because of this, many are discouraged from using them in coursework. In this section we outline some of the techniques that might be particularly useful in preparing assignments. At the end of this chapter there are some exercises with solutions so that you can practise the techniques and become more confident in their use in assignments. However, take care to remember the warning given on page 14.

5.1 Rounding of Figures

When economists deal with large numbers, such as the number of workers unemployed or total expenditure on imports in a particular year, these numbers are so large that they can never be perfectly accurate. For example, total expenditure on imports in a particular year runs to thousands of millions of pounds! Because of the amount involved, any attempt to measure total expenditure on imports is certain to contain errors and omissions. In other words, some expenditure on imports will have been incorrectly included while other expenditure will have been overlooked altogether.

Because these figures are not entirely accurate, economists *round* their estimates of them. But what does it mean to 'round' an estimate?
Consider a figure such as 10,476.

- Rounded to the nearest ten, this figure becomes, 10,480.
- Rounded to the nearest hundred, it becomes 10,500 and so on.

If you look at some of the data given in the sources discussed earlier you will notice that a great deal of data used by economists *is* rounded. You should have no reservations about using rounded data in your assignments. As long as data refers to the *same aggregate* and is rounded to the *same figure* you can apply the rules of simple arithmetic when dealing with it. For example, if you have the unemployment figures for two regions for the same period rounded to the nearest thousand, you can combine them to obtain an estimate of total unemployment in *both* regions. Similarly, you could divide this figure by two to obtain an estimate of the *average* rate of unemployment in *each* region.

5.2 Divisions of the Whole

Another technique that is often very useful in analysing economic data is to break it into divisions of the whole. This simply means that we use *fractions*, *decimals* or *percentages* to analyse the facts and figures we have collected.

FRACTIONS

You are probably very familiar with fractions, but if someone asked you to tell them *exactly* what a fraction is, how would you describe it? In fact, a fraction is simply part of a whole number. For example $\frac{1}{4}$ is a fourth of one. The upper part of the fraction (the number 1) is referred to as the *numerator* and the lower part (the number 4) is referred to as the *denominator*.

Fractions are easily calculated. For example, if we wish to know what fraction 1,000 is of 10,000, we simply divide 1,000 by 10,000. Thus 1,000/10,000 = 1/10.

DECIMALS

Decimals are much more common in the calculation and presentation of economic data than fractions. Strictly a decimal is a fraction with a denominator of 10, or some power of 10 such as 10^2, 10^3 and so on. This sounds very complicated but is actually quite easy.

To obtain a decimal from a fraction we simply divide the numerator by the denominator, adding noughts to the numerator as required. However, you must remember that when you add the first nought to the numerator, you must insert a decimal point in your answer. Fortunately most people have access to an electronic calculator which will perform the necessary arithmetic and give the answer as a decimal.

PERCENTAGES

A percentage simply means parts of a hundred. Thus 25 per cent is simply 25 parts of a hundred. To convert a decimal to a percentage simply multiply the decimal by 100. For example, if we express $\frac{1}{4}$ as a decimal we have 0.25. Multiplying this by 100 gives 25 per cent. This means that $\frac{1}{4}$ is 25 per cent of a whole.

In your assignment it is often useful to show fully your working for any calculations you include. We can set the above calculation out in the following way:

Fraction   Decimal   Percentage

$\frac{1}{4}$ = 0.25 = 0.25 × 100 = 25%

A common problem faced by students is how to measure the *percentage change* in a particular variable. To do this, simply take the *actual change*, divide it by the *original value*, and multiply the result by 100. For example, if the price of a good increases from £10 to £12, it is easy to work out the percentage change in price by following the instructions above:

Original price New price Change in price Percentage change in price

£10   £12   £12 − £10 = £2 $\frac{£2}{£10} \times 100 = 20\%$

Percentages are very useful in Economics, especially when measuring rates of growth or making comparisons. For example, if your assignment topic is an investigation into house prices in two different parts of your home town, you will almost certainly need to use percentages. Let us call these areas, Area 1 and Area 2 and let us assume we have the following information:

	Average House Prices	
	In Area 1 (£)	In Area 2 (£)
1989	80,000	60,000
1990	90,000	69,000

Thus, the average price of housing in Area 1 increased from £80,000 to £90,000 in the twelve months 1989 – 1990, and from £60,000 to £69,000 in Area 2. It is clear that the *absolute* increase, that is the actual amount by which house prices increased, was greater in Area 1 at £10,000, than in Area 2 at £9,000. However, house prices in 1989 were already higher in Area 1 than Area 2, and in order to make a proper comparison of these increases we need to calculate the *percentage* increase in house prices in both areas. We can set this calculation out for Area 1 in exactly the same way as the previous calculation:

	Original price	New price	Change in price	Percentage change in price
Area 1	£80,000	£90,000	£10,000	$\dfrac{£10,000}{£80,000} \times 100 = 12.5\%$
Area 2	£60,000	£69,000	£9,000	$\dfrac{£9,000}{£60,000} \times 100 = 15.0\%$

It is important to note here that the *absolute* size of any increase in prices is not necessarily a good guide to the *percentage* increase in prices. In this case the absolute increase in house prices was greater in Area 1 than Area 2, but the percentage increase was greater in Area 2 than in Area 1. To economists the percentage increase is far more important than the absolute increase. One reason for this is that it enables us to make comparisons. For example, the figures we are given imply that we would have made a greater return on our expenditure if we bought a house in Area 2 than if we bought a house in Area 1.

Sometimes percentages are worked out for us so that we can make comparisons. This is especially true of rates of interest charged on loans or earned on investments. We can see how easy it is to make comparisons when this information is readily available. For example, if you had £1,000 to invest and were offered a rate of interest on your investment of 5 per cent by one institution, and a rate of interest of 7.5 per cent on the same investment by another institution, where would you invest your £1,000?

Percentages are not only useful when making comparisons between variables, they are also extremely important when comparing changes *over time* in the rate of growth of a single variable. For example, you could use annual percentage increases to show changes in the average price of housing in a single area. You might then compare this with changes in interest rates, changes in income, or changes in unemployment to see if there is any relationship.

5.3 Averages

When comparing one variable with another, or when measuring changes in a given variable over time, economists frequently make use of *averages*. There are various ways of measuring an average, but the most commonly used measure is referred to by mathematicians as the *arithmetic mean*, or just the *mean*. This is simply the total of all values under consideration, divided by the number of values.

An example will make this clear. If a person's expenditure over a period of 5 days is:

Day	Amount spent (£)
1	2.5
2	4.0
3	1.3
4	2.0
5	0.2

Total expenditure over the five-day period is £10. If this is divided by 5 (the number of days) this gives us an average expenditure of £2 per day. In other words:

$$\text{Average daily expenditure} = \frac{£10}{5} = £2$$

5.4 Diagrams

BAR CHARTS

These are one of the most widely used techniques for presenting economic data. It is possible that you will want to use a *bar chart* in your assignment. It is therefore important for you to understand how to construct one and how to interpret the information it gives. However, it is also important for you to understand how to interpret a bar chart, since you are almost certain to come across them when you examine economic data.

Bar charts can either be drawn vertically or horizontally. Which is preferable is a matter of personal choice, though vertical bar charts are more commonly used. Whichever way you present information, it is important that you give your diagram a *title* and a *scale*. You should also ensure that the original *source* of your information is given.

A bar chart can be used to show the importance of the *different components of a given aggregate*. For example, we could use a bar chart to show the *proportion* of an individual's expenditure on a given day on different goods and services purchased. Thus, an individual's total purchases can be itemised as:

Bus Fares £1.20
Lunch £0.80
Stationery £1.25
Refreshments £0.75

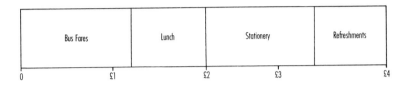

Fig 2.1
Bar chart

This can be represented in the form of a bar chart as in Figure 2.1. Bar charts are also useful when we wish to compare *different aggregates*, such as exports and imports, or if we wish to compare the way a single aggregate, such as population, has changed over time. Figure 2.2 and Table 2.4 gives an example. With respect to Figure 2.2, note the use of a zig-zag to break the 'Y'-axis, that is the axis showing total population, and the change in scale that this makes possible. Plot the data in Table 2.4 *without* a zig-zag break using a scale of 1cm = 10 million on the 'Y'-axis and you will soon see the advantage the zig-zag gives in making clear the changes that have occurred in population of the UK in each of the years illustrated. We think you will agree that breaking the 'Y'-axis with a zig-zag makes the diagram considerably clearer and easier to interpret by reducing it to a more manageable size.

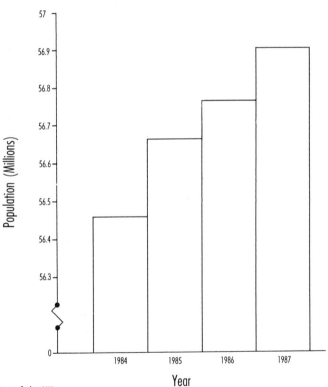

Fig 2.2
Bar chart of population of the UK

Table 2.4 Population of the UK

Year	Millions of persons
1984	56460
1985	56618
1986	56763
1987	56930

Source: Monthly Digest of Statistics, No 516, December 1988, HMSO.

This is a useful technique if your observations have a value which is considerably greater than zero, as in this case. You can also use this technique when plotting a *line graph* (see page 27 below). However, take care when you use or refer to data which is broken by a zig-zag. It can give a misleading impression of how quickly a variable is rising or falling. Compare the bar chart given here with the one you are asked to plot and you will see what we mean.

On first glance, bar charts seem fairly easy to understand. However, you should take very great care when comparing one bar chart with another. You must ensure that they illustrate the *same aggregate*. For example, if we have two bar charts showing population at different points in time, they are not strictly comparable if one shows the population of the UK while the other shows the population of Great Britain. You must also ensure that they use the same scales. These are of course elementary points. They are, nevertheless, easily neglected!

PIE CHARTS

These are also frequently used in Economics as a means of presenting data. The main purpose of a *pie chart* is to show the *relative* importance of the different components of a *given total*. You will probably have guessed that this means they give the same kind of information as Figure 2.1. This is indeed the case, but pie charts are a little more difficult to construct than bar charts! Despite this, they are easy to *understand*.

To construct a pie chart you will need a compass and a protractor. Let us use the information about personal expenditure given on page 25 as an example. First you must draw a circle of any radius – it must, of course, be big enough to enable you to illustrate the information you intend to illustrate! The circle represents the total. In our case it represents total spending by an individual on a given day. The problem now is to divide the circle into its component parts, that is expenditure on bus fares, lunch and so on. This is where you will need your protractor. There are 360° in a circle, and therefore each component of the circle has to be represented as a *proportion* of 360°. Refer to the information given on page 25 and you will see that total spending on this day was £4 of which £1.20 was spent on bus fares. We can calculate what percentage of total spending this represents:

$$\frac{£1.20}{£4.00} \times 100 = 30\%$$

This means that the segment of our pie chart which represents expenditure on *bus fares* is equal to 30 per cent of the area of the circle. To be able to draw this segment we must first multiply 360° by 30%:

$$\frac{30}{100} \times 360° = 108°$$

Now find the mid-point of the circle and draw a radius. Next, use your protractor to mark off an angle of 108° and draw another radius such that the angle between the two radii you have drawn is 108°.

To obtain the next segment of the pie-chart simply repeat the procedure. For example, as a percentage of total expenditure, *lunch* is equal to £0.80/£4.00 × 100 = 20 per cent. This means we require an angle of 20/100 × 360° = 72°. Taking your protractor and using one of the radii you have already drawn, mark off an angle 72°. Draw another radius such that the angle between the radius you have constructed and the one you have previously drawn, is 72°.

Figure 2.3 represents the expenditure of our individual as a pie chart. To help you we show the *angles* as well as the *percentage contribution* of each component.

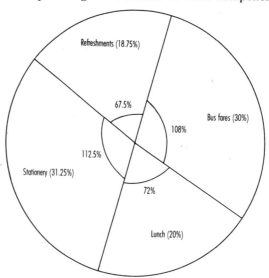

Fig 2.3
Pie chart

Although pie charts are widely used by economists to present information, there are several points you should bear in mind when constructing or interpreting them:

- Pie diagrams involve calculations which you should check before constructing your diagram.
- Check the accuracy of all angles before you mark off each segment of your diagram.
- Take care when comparing the *size* of different segments. It is not always easy to see when one segment is bigger than another. (The same is not true with bar charts!)
- Unless pie charts give actual figures in each segment, the value of the components of the pie chart are unknown. Similarly, unless figures are given, the percentage value of each component is unknown. (The same is not true of a bar chart where each component is represented against a scale!)

Pie charts should not be confused with Venn diagrams, an example of which is shown on page 42.

LINE GRAPHS

Again this is a widely-used technique to present information in Economics. The most frequently-used *line graph* is that which illustrates the behaviour of a particular variable over some period of time. Interest rates, the balance of payments, the rate of inflation and so on are all frequently illustrated using line graphs. When a variable is plotted over time we often refer to the graph as a *time graph* and we say that the data which the line graph illustrates is *time series* data.

Constructing line graphs is quite easy. Having collected the information you wish to plot, you must group it into pairs of points. These are referred to as *co-ordinates*. It is customary to plot the *dependent variable* on the vertical, or 'Y'-axis. But what do we mean by, 'the dependent variable'? In simple terms, the dependent variable is determined by, or *depends upon*, another variable. Thus, if we plot expenditure on imports for the UK over a number of years, import expenditure is the dependent variable because its value depends on which year we consider. However, the opposite is not true; the year we consider is unaffected by import expenditure! Similarly, if we plot total output against number of hours worked, total output is the dependent variable, since its value depends on the number of hours worked. Remember, whenever any variable is plotted against time; time is always the *independent variable*. This tells you that time is always plotted along the 'X'-axis.

Next you must choose a scale for each of your axes. The point at which your axes cross is referred to as the *origin* and it is usual for all variables to have a value of zero at the origin. Bearing this in mind your scale should be large enough to make clear the way in which the variable you are plotting has behaved over time. Sometimes the choice of a scale is easy, but what if the first observation you wish to plot has a value of several thousand million pounds? This would be the case if you were plotting UK expenditure on consumer goods and services over time. Some information on the way this has changed over time is given in Table 2.5, and one way in which it can be plotted so as to indicate the changes that have occurred over the time period considered, is shown in Figure 2.4. Here again, note the use of a zig-zag to break the 'Y'-axis enabling us to show the range £62m – £75m. Without the zig-zag, our line graph would occupy such a small proportion of the diagram it would be less clear and considerably more difficult to interpret.

Table 2.5
Quarterly expenditure in £m of UK consumers.

1987	Q1	62645
	Q2	63845
	Q3	66050
	Q4	68150
1988	Q1	69884
	Q2	71207
	Q3	73832

Source: Economic Trends, No 422, December 1988, HMSO.

Fig 2.4
Line graph of quarterly expenditure of UK consumers

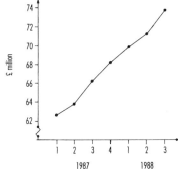

As previously explained, line graphs are a commonly-used technique for presenting certain types of economic data, especially time series data, that is, data with time on one axis. Line graphs are popular because they highlight *trends* and *relationships* in data that are not so easy to spot if data is simply presented in the form of a table. When constructing your own line graphs remember the following points of good practice:

- Label your axes showing clearly the units of measurement. For example, the variable on your 'X'-axis might be time and this might be measured in quarters of a year as in Figure 2.4.
- Give the original source of the information plotted.
- Give the graph a title indicating what it shows.
- Plot the *independent variable* on the 'X'-axis. This variable should be the one that is changed to assess the impact on a different (*dependent*) variable.
- Plot the *dependent variable* on the 'Y'-axis.
- Choose a scale that enables you to identify changes in the dependent variable.
- When the same axes are used to plot more than one graph, draw each graph in a *different colour* so that they are easily distinguished. Remember to include a *key* showing which variable is shown by which graph.

Interpolation

Sometimes we require information about a particular variable that is not available. For example, if you look at Figure 2.4, this shows the quarterly expenditure of consumers in the UK. We can use this graph to *estimate* expenditure in any particular *month* for the period illustrated. We might wish to estimate consumer's expenditure in the seventh month of 1988. To do this we first draw a line from the 'X'-axis one third of the distance between quarter 2 and quarter 3, to the graph of consumer's expenditure, taking care to ensure that this line is parallel to the 'Y'-axis. From the point where this line meets the graph we draw another line to the 'Y'-axis, this time taking care to ensure that the line is parallel to the 'X'-axis. The point where this line meets the 'Y'-axis gives us our *estimate* of consumer's expenditure for the seventh month of 1988. In this case consumer's expenditure is estimated to be £72082m (see Fig 2.5). This procedure is referred to as *interpolation* and it provides a means of extracting information from a graph *between* points. Question 7 on page 32 provides you with an opportunity to test your ability at interpolation.

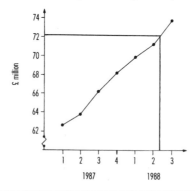

Extrapolation

It is possible to use some graphs to predict future values of a variable. Of course these estimates might not always be reliable but if a *clear trend* can be identified on a graph then, at least for predictions in the near future, graphs might be a suitable starting point. All that happens in the case of *extrapolation* is that the graph is continued several periods into the future, taking care to follow the pattern established in earlier periods.

UNIT 6 METHODS OF INVESTIGATION

We have already discussed the use of questionnaires on pages 19–22. Here we concentrate on the different approaches to *investigative work*.

6.1 Formulating a Hypothesis

As we mentioned at the beginning of this chapter, when carrying out research, practising economists frequently begin by formulating a *hypothesis*. A hypothesis is simply an attempt to explain a particular occurrence, or to offer a possible answer to a particular question. For example, the question might be posed, 'Why is the South East of England more prosperous than the North East?' Another question might be, 'Why do firms in the same industry sometimes locate in the same area?' There are many possible answers to these questions, but

> **Take care in phrasing your hypothesis.**

not all of them will necessarily be correct. How do we decide if one answer is correct and another incorrect?

One way of answering questions of the type given above is to *formulate a hypothesis*, and then to carry out research to *test* whether the hypothesis is correct. To do this, your hypothesis should be phrased in such a way that it gives you the chance of providing a possible response to the issue or question. Thus, if you are considering why firms in the same industry sometimes locate in the same area, your hypothesis might be: 'Firms in the same industry sometimes locate close to each other because of the availability of *external economies of scale*'. You can then use your information or analysis to say how far you agree or disagree with this hypothesis.

Unless you are directed by your teacher, or by the Examining Group whose paper you are preparing for, to investigate a particular topic, you must first decide *which part of the syllabus* you are going to study. It is sometimes a good idea to investigate an *industry* or a *market*, such as the housing market, in your home town. The main advantage of this is, of course, that an adequate supply of *data* is almost certain to be readily available.

Even if you have decided to carry out an investigation into the housing market or into the importance of external economies of scale in some local industry, you still have to decide where to begin and what sort of hypothesis to test. With respect to the property market, if you live in a large town an obvious area to focus on is what determines the price of a particular type of house in different parts of the town. Information is readily available from the local newspaper and from the various estate agents.

6.2 Testing your Hypothesis

> Relate the data collected to simple economic theory.

Take care when you gather this information; simply lumping it together without *analysing* it will gain you little, if any, credit. In particular, you should try and link the information you gather to what you have learned from studying economics about the way in which prices are determined. Concentrate especially on using supply and demand analysis to explain price differences for the same type of housing. This is not an easy task but, if done well, it will almost certainly gain much credit. Look at the way information is analysed in the model assignments given in Chapter 3. A careful examination of these should help you to see what we mean.

With respect to the *housing market*, a major determinant of price is the *area* in which the property is located. Some areas are considered more desirable than others. This will certainly influence supply of, and demand for, housing in different areas, but what makes one area more desirable than another?

Another factor influencing the price of an individual house is its *outlook*. For example, most people prefer *privacy* at home, so if a house has a *private, secluded*, position this will be an advantage over a house which is *overlooked* by neighbouring property.

The *state of the house* will be another factor. A house in good state of repair will have an advantage over a house in need of repair, redecoration, and so on.

> Does the evidence support or conflict with your hypothesis?

You might formulate a hypothesis about house prices such as: 'Within the town of . . . the most important factor determining the price of a particular house is the part of the town in which it is located'. Whether this statement is true or not can be checked against the *evidence*, to see if it offers a reasonable explanation of why house prices vary in different parts of the town. In other words, you can use the evidence to test whether your hypothesis is correct. If your hypothesis *is* supported by the evidence, that is similar houses are more expensive in some areas than in others, then we say that the hypothesis is *accepted*. On the other hand, if your hypothesis *is not* supported by the evidence, we say the hypothesis is *rejected*.

This seems simple enough, but before you can accept or reject a hypothesis you must take great care. In carrying out investigations aimed at testing a hypothesis you must make sure that you examine *all* of the available information. You cannot limit the evidence you study to that which supports your own view. If you do this you will accept hypotheses which are not really supported by all of the facts, and which should therefore be rejected!

> the golden rule for testing a hypothesis

Of course this does *not* necessarily mean that all of the information you have gathered will be useful. Sometimes when you gather information it is not always easy to see whether it will be useful, or the way in which you will use it, in your assignment. The golden rule to remember is that, when testing a hypothesis, *all relevant information must be considered*.

> Avoid problems by planning ahead.

One of your first tasks should therefore be to decide *how much* of the information you have gathered you are going to include in your investigation. This means looking very carefully at your hypothesis and thinking about how much of the information is *useful* or *relevant* to the way you are going to develop your assignment. Next, you must think about how you are going to *use* the information you have decided to include. To do this you must *plan* the way in which your assignment will be presented.

PLANNING

Planning your work is not an easy task. If it is done thoroughly it might even take several hours! Nevertheless, work that is well planned at the outset is easier to write and this will save a considerable amount of time and effort later. Write down the way you plan to write your project in as much detail as you think necessary. Remember, writing up a whole assignment is likely to take several days at least, and might even take several weeks, especially if you are trying to complete other assignments at the same time. Unless you make a detailed plan, outlining your ideas and the way you intend developing them, it is possible that as you proceed through your coursework you will not remember clearly what you intended to investigate or write about a particular point when you come to deal with it.

In planning your work remember that you can use data to *demonstrate* a variety of important *skills*. For example, you can demonstrate *numerate skills*, the ability to *understand an argument* and to *interpret information* and so on. Remember though, data must be relevant and must be supported by a discussion of the issues it illustrates.

UNIT 7 — APPLYING ECONOMIC CONCEPTS, THEORIES AND IDEAS

A different way of approaching coursework is to try to *apply* economic concepts and theories to particular situations. Such an approach need not necessarily involve a vast amount of time in gathering information and data. Indeed, in some cases all of the data you require will be readily available around your own home. For example, you might consider the cost of running a household consumer durable such as a freezer or a motor car.

7.1 Assignment: Running a family car

Consider the *cost of running a typical family car*. Even if you do not own a car you could obtain all of the information you will require for an assignment of this nature from banks, car dealers, adverts in weekly and monthly car magazines and so on.

DEFINING TYPES OF COST

You could begin your assignment by *defining* some of the terms you are going to use such as *opportunity* cost, *fixed* cost, *variable* cost, *average fixed* cost, *average variable* cost, *average total* cost and so on.

CONSIDERING EACH TYPE OF COST

You could then consider *each type* of cost in terms of running a family motor car.

Opportunity cost

Beginning with *opportunity cost* you could consider the alternatives such as a re-fitted kitchen or a family holiday, that might have been bought with the money used to purchase the motor car, or the interest that is forgone when money is spent rather than being placed in a savings account. If all or part of the money is borrowed, interest will be charged on the loan. Here again, the money used to pay interest charges could have been used to purchase something else, or it might have been saved, in which case it would earn interest. In addition, when we use a car we incur other costs such as petrol, insurance and so on. Again, these expenditures mean that money spent running the car is not available for the purchase of other things. Judged in these terms the opportunity cost of owning and running a car is quite substantial for most of us!

Fixed cost

Next you might consider the *fixed costs* of owning and running a motor car. In theory, fixed costs are easy to define, but in practice it is not always easy to identify whether a cost is fixed or variable. You should therefore take particular care here. Economists define fixed costs as those costs which must be paid whether an asset is used or not and which do not change regardless of how often an asset is used. Some of the fixed costs of owning a car include *taxation, insurance, interest on borrowed funds* and, most important of all for the majority of cars, *depreciation*. The longer you own a car and the more miles it covers, the lower its resale value. Looking at the prices of second-hand cars similar to your own family car and comparing these with the price of a new model of the same car therefore provides one possible way of estimating depreciation. You could develop this idea further and in estimating depreciation you might try to assesss the loss in *real terms*, that is, after allowing for the effect of inflation on the second-hand value of the car from the time it was initially purchased, as well as the loss in *nominal terms*.

Variable cost

In estimating the *variable costs* of running the car, an obvious point to focus on is the difference in the number of miles per gallon (or litre) that is achieved when driving at different speeds. In particular, fewer miles per gallon are achieved on short journeys or when driving in towns or cities, than are achieved on longer journeys.

PRESENTING DATA

Much of what was written earlier (see pages 22–8) about the presentation of data when explaining the results of hypothesis testing is relevant here. You could use *line graphs* to illustrate the behaviour of costs such as *average variable costs per mile*, *average fixed costs per mile* and so on. You could also *compare* the importance of the different variable costs incurred on a given journey by using a *bar chart* or a *pie chart*.

UNIT 8 SKILLS TO CONCENTRATE ON

A full explanation of the skills to be developed when studying GCSE Economics is given on pages 2–5. As previously explained, these skills are known as the *assessment objectives* and they are graded into *levels of performance*. In other words, they are used to decide how many marks an assignment is to be awarded. The different Examination Groups outline these skills in different ways, but there is clearly a great deal of similarity between them.

Some of these skills are easier to demonstrate than others. It is particularly important to demonstrate an ability to *apply knowledge*, to *analyse information* and to *make reasoned judgements*.

- **Applying knowledge** This basically means *using economic concepts* and *theories* to explain the behaviour of individuals, groups, firms and so on. For example, on page 30 it was suggested that a possible coursework topic might be an investigation into the cost of running a family car. Here, the application of knowledge would be in the *identification* of costs such as petrol, depreciation and so on.
- **Analysing information** Analysis is more complex. It is a skill that can be demonstrated in several ways:
  - It might involve an explanation of the *relationship* that exists between different variables which form part of an investigation.
  - It might involve identifying the main *assumptions* on which a particular argument is based.
  - It might involve an *explanation* of the causes of some particular event. For example, why does the average fixed cost of running a motor car fall continuously as more miles are covered?
- **Making reasoned judgements** The ability to make reasoned judgements involves *recognising* the *accuracy* or *reliability* of some information compared with other information. It also means the ability to distinguish matters of opinion from matters of fact. For example, it is a matter of *opinion* whether running a family car provides good value for money, but it is a matter of *fact* that a particular car cost £8,000 to buy when it was originally purchased!

UNIT 9 PRACTICE QUESTIONS

Here are some questions designed to test your ability to use the arithmetical and statistical techniques discussed in the text. The answers are given below. If you disagree with any of the answers given in the book, have a second try at the question. If you still disagree and you wish to use the technique in your assignment, ask your teacher for help.

1   Round the following figures to the nearest:
    a) whole number; b) ten; c) hundred; d) thousand.
    i) 10,435.67; ii) 150,376.89; iii) 243,999.24

2   If the rate of inflation per quarter in a particular economy for each of four quarters is: Q1 4.5 per cent, Q2 2.3 per cent, Q3 5.2 per cent Q4 3.4 per cent, what is:
    a) The average quarterly rate of inflation for the whole period?
    b) The average rate of inflation for the first two quarters and the last two quarters?
    c) The estimated rate of inflation in i) the fifth month; ii) the seventh month?

3   The price of good A in four quarters of the same year was; Q1 £10; Q2 £12; Q3 £15; Q4 £12. Calculate the percentage change in the price of good A between: i) Q1 – Q2, ii) Q2 – Q3, iii) Q3 – Q4, iv) Q1 – Q3.

Table 2.6 shows the annual rate of inflation in the UK for certain years.

Table 2.6

Year	Rate of inflation (per cent)
1983	4.6
1984	5.0
1985	6.1
1986	3.4
1987	4.2
1988	4.9

Source: Economic Trends, No 424 February 1989, HMSO.

4   Use this information to draw a bar chart showing the annual rate of inflation for each of the year's given.

5   Using the information in Table 2.6, draw a line graph showing movements in the annual rate of inflation for each of the years given.

6   Would the information in Table 2.6 be suitable for constructing a pie diagram? Explain your answer.

7   The information given in Table 2.7 shows the percentage share in each of the standard categories of Total Final Expenditure in the UK for the third quarter of 1988. Use this information to construct a pie chart.

Table 2.7
Total Final Expenditure
(Percentage shares in each category)

	Consumers' Expenditure	Exports of Goods and Services	Gross Fixed Investment	General Government Consumption
1988 Q1	50.8	19.4	14.2	15.7

Source: Economic Trends, No 422 December 1988, HMSO.

UNIT 10 ANSWERS TO EXERCISES

1. a) i) 10,436   ii) 150,377   iii) 243,999
   b) i) 10,440   ii) 150,380   iii) 244,000
   c) i) 10,400   ii) 150,400   iii) 244,000
   d) i) 10,000   ii) 150,000   iii) 244,000

2. a) 3,85%; b) 3.4% and 4.3%; c) 3.03% and 3.27%

3. i) $\dfrac{£12 - £10}{£10} \times 100 = 20\%$ ii) $\dfrac{£15 - £12}{£12} \times 100 = 25\%$

   iii) $\dfrac{£12 - £15}{£15} \times 100 = 20\%$ (fall)   iv) $\dfrac{£15 - £10}{£10} \times 100 = 50\%$

4. See Fig 2.6

5. See Fig 2.7

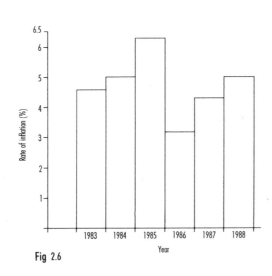

Fig 2.6

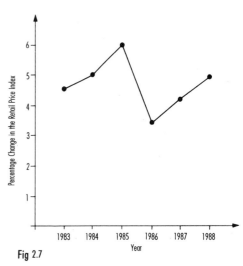

Fig 2.7

6. No, because it is time series data. A pie chart can only be constructed when we have the values of the different components of a given total.

7. See Fig 2.8

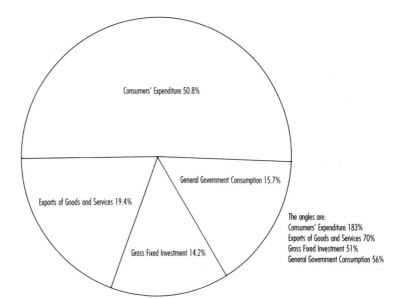

Fig 2.8

PRESENTING AN ASSIGNMENT

Let us look at the stages involved in completing a coursework assignment. We will follow the steps taken by two 'model' students.

Our first student is Sally, who is in the Sixth Form at the Burnt Mill High School, Longmanton. Her Economics teacher is Mr. Keynes.

UNIT 1 — SALLY'S ASSIGNMENT

1.1 Stage 1: Choosing a Topic

Sally gave this a lot of thought, and discussed various possibilities with Mr. Keynes. He asked her to select a general area of the syllabus which she found interesting, and where she could collect information fairly easily. As Sally is a Sixth Form student, she will be sitting GCSE after only one year: she therefore realised that she did not have as much time as she would have liked and therefore wanted a topic which is taught fairly early in the course. Sally chose 'banking'.

1.2 Stage 2: Choosing a Title

Mr. Keynes prefers titles which enable his students to investigate things at first hand, rather than read about them second-hand from books.
Sally had noticed that banking services were being very heavily advertised on television. Slogans such as 'the listening bank', 'the bank that likes to say yes', and 'a new type of bank account' were becoming very familiar to everyone. She also discovered that most of her friends had savings accounts, to which they had been attracted by various special offers and gimmicks, and she knew that some of the Sixth Formers even had their own current accounts with cashcards and cheque-books. She chose as her title:

'An Economic Survey of the Banking Services Available to the Citizens of Longmanton'.

This would enable her to collect information from local banks and building societies, and there was obviously great potential for using questionnaires in surveying her family and friends.

1.3 Stage 3: Taking Aim

Sally realised that she needed to conduct an 'Economic' survey, otherwise the assignment could become purely *descriptive*. She decided that she would inject 'Economics' into her work by looking at the themes of 'consumer choice' and 'competition' in banking.
Sally had noticed that the market for current accounts was becoming more and more competitive, with many thousands of pounds being spent on advertising. While building societies had begun offering current accounts, banks had begun advertising their mortgage services. She therefore decided that her aim was to test the following hypothesis:

Increased competition has made banks become more like building societies and building societies become more like banks.

1.4 Stage 4: Planning

What Sally now needed was to organise her thoughts on how her assignment would be organised. She sat down and drew up a *synopsis*. A synopsis is a 'battle plan' which gives you a *framework*: around this basic structure you can build up your assignment. The synopsis need not be adhered to rigidly; it can be modified as you go, but at least it helps you to map out your work in advance.

SALLY'S SYNOPSIS

- An outline of the traditional functions of banks and building societies, and the services they provide.
- The local scene. Sketch map showing the position of banks and building societies in Longmanton town centre (some attempt to explain these locations).
- Details of the banking services offered to the citizens of Longmanton (concentrating on recent changes in current accounts).
- Recent changes in banking, and an economic analysis of the reasons for these changes.
- Comments on the similarities and differences between banks and building societies.
- Conclusions.

1.5 Stage 5: Preparation

Mr. Keynes advised that an essential preparation is to read the relevant sections in an Economics textbook. This gives the theoretical background to a topic, and helps to study the topic from an economist's point of view.

Sally had no difficulty in finding textbook material on banking; however, she did notice that information does tend to go out of date rather quickly. Luckily, the banks are always pleased to supply leaflets and other publicity material. Mr. Keynes also drew Sally's attention to some booklets from the Building Societies Association and the Banking Information Service which were available in school.

1.6 Stage 6: Gathering Information

Sally produced a sketch map of her town centre, marking on it the positions of branches of banks and building societies. She then collected booklets from each of the branches, looking in particular for information relevant to her title and hypothesis. She therefore concentrated on information about current accounts, credit cards, loans and mortgages. She also monitored the television and press for news items and advertisements relating to banks and building societies, looking in particular for how often they advertised and who the advertisements were aimed at.

Sally also designed a short and simple questionnaire aimed at discovering to what extent Sixth formers used banks and building societies.

1.7 Stage 7: Using Information

By now Sally had collected quite a bit of information. It was necessary to sift through it and sort out the pieces which were of most use. She found it important to be selective; for example, she wished to concentrate on current accounts, loans and mortgage services, and she was therefore able to ignore information on, say, insurance services. She looked again at her synopsis, and decided how to relate the information she had gathered to each section of the assignment.

1.8 Stage 8: Writing and Presentation

Mr. Keynes is very keen on presentation. He gives each student a 'Format' which he expects them to follow as far as possible. Mr. Keynes' format appears as follows:

1. TITLE PAGE
2. CONTENTS PAGE
3. INTRODUCTION
4. TEXT
5. CONCLUSIONS AND EVALUATION
6. ACKNOWLEDGEMENTS AND BIBLIOGRAPHY
7. DECLARATION
8. APPENDIX

THE TITLE PAGE

It is obvious that this gives the title of the assignment; what is not so obvious is the reason why so many candidates forget to write one. This is very irritating for teachers and examiners alike.

CONTENTS PAGE

This lists the sections and chapters of the assignment, and states the page number where each one starts. Obviously, for the contents page to be of any use to the reader, the pages of the assignment must be numbered.

AN INTRODUCTION

The introduction should state the aims of the assignment, and should therefore contain a hypothesis or pose a question.

THE TEXT

This is the main section of the assignment, and may be broken down into several chapters; these chapters may themselves be broken down into sub-chapters, each with a sub-heading. It is important that these pieces should be fitted together in a logical order.

When presenting *statistics*, examiners like to see a variety of presentation techniques such as pie-charts, bar diagrams and graphs. Make sure that any diagrams of this sort are neatly drawn and labelled, and that they are relevant to the text.

CONCLUSIONS AND EVALUATION

Having begun with a hypothesis or question it is essential to come to some *conclusions*. If the results of the research are inconclusive, then recognise this fact and say so. It is worth spending some time writing this section; very often an examiner will find that it is the *way* in which a candidate draws conclusions which distinguishes a good assignment from one that is run-of-the-mill.

It is also worthwhile *evaluating* the whole exercise: stating whether doing the assignment was an enjoyable experience, whether anything worthwhile was learned, whether the results were predictable or unexpected, and whether the aims have been achieved. It is also a good idea to comment on the effectiveness of different research methods used, on any problems encountered, and on which sources of information were most useful.

ACKNOWLEDGEMENTS AND BIBLIOGRAPHY

It is necessary to make a list of any books and articles which have been used, and include a note of thanks to anyone who helped, for instance, those people who filled in your questionnaires.

DECLARATION

Candidates should state that the assignment is their own work, and sign this declaration.

APPENDIX

This is a collection of pages at the end of the assignment which contains detailed information which was not included in the main section. For instance, if questionnaires were used, there should be an outline of the questions asked and an analysis of the results in the main section; the 'raw data' (completed questionnaires) can be put in the Appendix. This avoids including so much information in the main section that it becomes clumsy and difficult to read.

UNIT 2 EXTRACTS FROM SALLY'S ASSIGNMENT

An Economic Survey
of the Banking Services
Available to the Citizens of
Longmanton

Chapter 1: Introduction

Banking is an important part of the study of Economics. For many years banking in Britain has been dominated by the 'Big Four':

Barclays, Lloyds
National Westminster, Midland.

These banks have branches in the High Street of any reasonably-sized town, and Longmanton is no exception. These banks are known as 'Commercial Banks' (to avoid confusion with Merchant Banks and the Central Bank, which is the Bank of England). They are also known as the Clearing Banks, because they belong to the London Clearing House, which is an organisation set up in order to help banks settle their debts with each other by clearing each other's cheques.

The main functions of Commercial Banks are as follows:

(1) Acceptance of deposits

This is probably the oldest function. The first banks were operated three centuries ago by goldsmiths and jewellers. They possessed strongrooms and safes, and during the English Civil War rich families who were fearful for the future deposited valuables such as gold for safe-keeping. The goldsmiths issued written receipts: the first 'pound note' was therefore a paper receipt for a pound (in weight) of gold. When the depositors had to pay a debt, very often the creditor would accept the paper receipt to a gold deposit rather than require payment in gold. Today, banks accept money for safe-keeping (it is much safer to keep money at the bank rather than under the bed in a shoebox), and they also offer strongboxes where jewellery, important documents, and other valuables can be stored.

(2) Transfer of deposits

A bank note is legally a 'promise to pay', whereas a cheque is an 'instruction to transfer'. When Mr. A writes a cheque to Miss B, the bank transfers money from one account to the other.

The cheque system has long been the main method of transferring funds. However, computerisation now means that 'non-paper' transfers are becoming more widely used. It is possible to foresee the day when plastic cards will replace both banknotes and cheques, but at the present time the current account with a chequebook is still a very important part of banking.

(3) Lending money

When money is deposited and people use cheques to pay bills to each other, the banks find that they have spare funds which they can lend to people who wish to borrow.

An overdraft arrangement enables an account holder to go 'into the red': to spend more than he or she has in the account. This is usually for some very short-term purpose, for example, to pay an unexpectedly high winter gas bill. This is the cheapest method of borrowing from a bank, because interest is paid only on the amount outstanding at the end of each day.

A loan is for a longer-term purpose, such as the purchase of a new car or a house extension (personal loans) or for factory investment (business loans). Unlike what happens with an overdraft, the borrower does not 'go into the red' by spending more than the amount in the account. Instead, the bank credits the borrower's account with the amount of the loan, and debits the repayment each month. The cost is higher than for an overdraft, because interest is paid on the whole amount borrowed, not just on the amount outstanding at the end of each day. Today, interest paid on overdrafts and loans provide the main source of bank profits. It is quite surprising to realise that the average manager of a local bank is likely to be responsible for the lending of millions of pounds to families and firms.

Other banking institutions

As well as the 'Big Four' banks, the following institutions in Longmanton also offer banking services:

(1) The Trustee Savings Bank (TSB)

There used to be hundreds of local Trustee Banks, owned by their members. The TSB is now a large Public Limited Company covering the whole country.

(2) National Girobank

This bank is operated by the Post Office, which has the advantages of longer opening hours than commercial banks, and easy access to the public through main and sub-post offices.

(3) The Cooperative Bank

There is no separate branch of this in Longmanton, but there is a bank within 'Leo's' superstore operated by Cooperative Retail Services.

(4) The following Building Societies have branches in Longmanton: Nationwide Anglia; Abbey National; Alliance and Leicester.
Empty shop units in the town centre are currently being renovated for conversion into branches of another two societies: Halifax and Britannia. In addition to these branches, local estate agents act as agencies for another three or four building societies.

Functions of Building Societies

The traditional function of Building Societies has been to accept deposits from people saving for house purchases, and to offer long-term loans known as 'mortgages' to people buying houses.
Building societies have shareholders, although they operate differently from the shareholders of companies. Each shareholder has only one vote in electing directors, so no one person can control the society by holding a large number of shares. Shares cannot be sold, and instead of a dividend, shareholders receive an agreed rate of interest. All profits are ploughed back into the society.
In order to obtain funds to lend for house purchase, societies offer savings accounts to the many small savers who require a safe investment with a good rate of interest.

My hypothesis

In recent years building societies have started competing more directly with the commercial banks, while commercial banks have been much more willing than before to offer mortgages. I have noticed this happening in Longmanton, and I therefore intend to use this assignment to test the following hypothesis:

> Increased competition has made banks more like building societies and building societies more like banks.

Chapter 2: The local banking scene

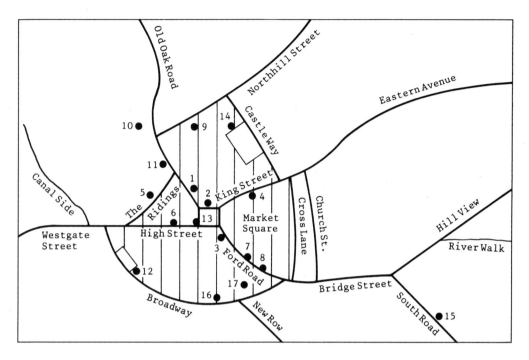

Fig 3.1

KEY
Main Shopping Area
1 Lloyds Bank
2 Midland Bank
3 Nat. West Bank
4 Barclays Bank
5 Natinwide Anglia (Old Premises)
6 Nationwide Anglia (New Premises opening Mar 1989)
7 Abbey National
8 Alliance & Leicester
9 TSB
10 Railway Station
11 Bus Station
12 CO-OP Superstore (with CO-OP Bank)
13 Post Office (with National Girobank)
14 Car Park
15 Burnt Mill High School
16 Site of Halifax
17 Site of Britannia – Due to open soon

In Longmanton, the commercial banks are grouped around the town centre (see Fig 3.1). They have dominated the banking scene for many years. They are well established, and have acquired prime sites at the centre of local commercial life.

The building societies are relative newcomers and traditionally have provided a more specialised service, so they are located in less-central positions, but as property has become available nearer to the centre the more 'go-getting' and competitive societies have moved in, often leaving smaller premises for larger units.

Current accounts

A current account is not used for long-term saving. It is used for everyday transactions which require withdrawal and transfer of funds on demand (without any period of notice). Current accounts have traditionally been offered by the commercial banks, and not by other institutions such as building societies. The current accounts offered by the commercial banks have usually had the following features:

(a) Transfer of deposits by cheque.
(b) Bank charges for each transfer.
(c) No interest on credit balances.
(d) Other optional services, such as cheque guarantee cards, electronic cash cards and credit cards.

The following chart (Fig 3.2) summarises the main current account services available to the citizens of Longmanton. You can see that the traditional scene has changed. In compiling this chart I have concentrated on the newer types of current account, which offer interest to the customer. This is something which the big four banks resisted for many years, until they were forced to introduce it by competition from some of the building societies. The broadening of the range of services offered by the building societies is also forcing the banks to consider the possibility of 'free' banking, that is, the abolition of bank charges on current accounts.

Note: The services available are changing rapidly, and might be different now from the time of the survey.

Bank/Building Society	Current Account with Cheque Book - Ordinary	Current Account with Cheque Book - Interest-bearing	Credit Card(s)	Automatic Teller Machine (ATM) Cash Card
Lloyds	✓	✓	✓	✓
Barclays	✓	✓	✓	✓
Midland	✓	✓	✓	✓
Nat West	✓	✓	✓	✓
Abbey National	-	✓	-	✓
Nationwide Anglia	-	✓	-	✓
Alliance & Leicester	-	-	-	✓
TSB	✓	-	✓	✓
CO-OP	-	✓	✓	-
Nat. Giro Bank	✓	-	-	✓

Fig 3.2
Availability of Current Account services in Longmanton

Chapter 3: Current trends affecting Banks and Building Societies

(a) Banks and Building Societies

British banks are Public Limited Companies: they exist in order to carry out the functions I have described earlier, but they also exist to make a profit for their shareholders. Building Societies, on the other hand, were established as 'mutual' organisations, owned by their members (savers and borrowers), on a non-profit making basis.

(b) The growth of owner-occupation

At the beginning of this century, 90% of the housing stock was privately rented, and most of the remainder was owner-occupied. During the First World War the Prime Minister, Lloyd-George, introduced rent restrictions on private landlords which continued into peace-time. He also said that Britain needed 'homes for heroes' and passed a law called the 'Addison Act' which enabled local councils to build houses to rent.
The 1920s and 1930s are known by economists as the Great Depression, but at least one sector of the economy was actually booming: private house-building, especially in the suburbs of London and large cities. New road-building schemes (and, in London, the extension of the Metropolitan Line) gave easier access into towns and cities from their suburbs and encouraged people to move from the urban areas into suburbia. Planning laws allowed 'ribbon development' (rows of houses on either side of a new road). The general recession caused low interest rates, and these together with government subsidies, the invention of the 'semi-detatched' house, and keen competition among housebuilders and speculators to acquire land and develop housing estates encouraged the building of houses for owner occupation.
This trend continued and accelerated with the higher incomes and living standards of the post-war period. An important influence on UK home ownership

has been the government concession of tax relief on mortgage interest repayments. Figure 3.3 shows how home ownership trends have developed. Britain has a higher proportion of home ownership than other European countries where private renting is much more common. In most countries a variety of institutions lend money for house-purchase. In Britain, Building Societies for many years dominated the housing finance market providing nearly 90% of the loans. Today, the banks have increased their share of these loans, and now offer mortgages on demand. Insurance companies also have a strong interest in the mortgage market, because more and more people are using endowment mortgages. In this case, with-profits life insurance is used to help repay the mortgage debt when the policy matures. The whole market has therefore become much more competitive.

Changes since 1986
1. Sales of Council Houses
2. Growth of Housing Associations
3. Abolition of Fair Rent Legislation

Sources: Building Societies Association, Social Trends

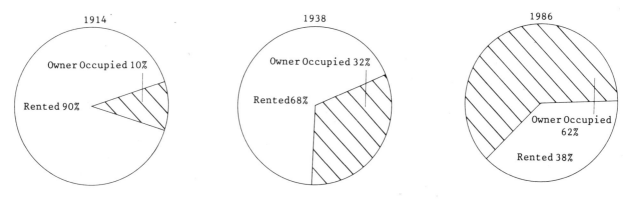

Fig 3.3

Changes in Legislation

During the 1970s and 1980s several government measures tried to encourage competition between banks and discourage the big banks from acting like a cartel (jointly fixing interest rates so that all the banks had equal rates).
During the late 1980s the 'Big Bang' occurred on the Stock Market, with repercussions in all financial services. The sale of council houses, rising incomes, and rising interest rates all occurred together with an incredibly rapid increase in house prices. Thus the banks were encouraged to enter the highly profitable mortgage market, while the Financial Services Act made it possible for Building Societies to offer a much wider range of banking services. It also enabled societies to take steps towards becoming Public Limited Companies if they wished.

New Technology

There is a trend towards a cashless society, and some people think that bank-notes and cheques will eventually disappear. It is hard to imagine life without notes and coins, but cheques are a different matter. Credit cards, electronic payments and cash dispensers could easily make cheques a thing of the past. The banks would welcome this, as the handling of millions of pieces of paper is expensive and time-consuming. It would be much simpler for the banks if all payments were made by bits of plastic linked to computers.
While some building societies already offer chequebooks and current accounts, the capital costs of setting up a cheque clearing system are, in economic jargon a 'barrier to entry' preventing many societies from competing in this market. Many building societies are probably waiting in the wings, hoping to avoid the chequebook generation and aiming for the electronic generation.
Perhaps this helps to explain why banks are so keen to attract younger customers. I have noticed that in my school many students have savings accounts. Some have collected many free gifts such as piggy-banks and pocket calculators by opening accounts at more than one bank.

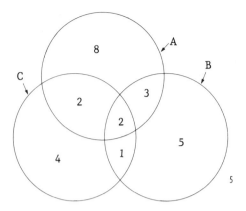

Fig 3.4

A = Post Office Account
B = Building Society Account
C = Bank Account
Of the sample of 30 Sixth-Formers
5 had no Account at all
15 had a Post Office Account
11 had a Building Society Account
9 had a Bank Account
The diagram shows that 8 people had an Account with two or more of the institutions (including 2 people with all three types of Account).

The Venn Diagram in Figure 3.4 illustrates the results of a survey I carried out among thirty Sixth-Formers at Burnt Mill High School chosen at random. I have heard it said that once people open an account they tend to stick with the same bank for life. One of the commercial banks comes into our school twice a week to help students operate a 'school bank'. This bank has 200 members at our school. Let us say that 100 of these members stay with this bank for life. If, of these customers, 50 take out a £50,000 mortgage, then that gives the bank potential business worth at least a quarter of a million pounds! Since this figure does not include interest payments, and makes no allowance for inflation, it is a conservative estimate. Little wonder then that these huge corporations can spare the time to help operate school banks.

Chapter 4: Conclusions

There is no doubt that banks and building societies are becoming much more similar and much more competitive. Banking was an 'oligopoly' (a market dominated by a handful of suppliers), but this is unlikely to continue. While I was writing up this assignment a real battle developed between the banks and building societies to keep existing customers and poach new customers from their rivals. The main weapons being used were the offer of 'free' banking (abolishing charges on current accounts), together with the offer of interest on current accounts.

The Midland bank began heavy TV advertising of its Vector account, along with a 'junior' version of the account. The second advertisement was clearly aimed at younger viewers. Indeed the script was almost identical to that of the commercial for Vector, and the actor playing the part of the customer mentioned that his 'older brother' was the one who opened the Vector account. One curious thing which occurred to me was that on TV it usually seems to be a male who is opening an account. In my research I did not notice that males were any more likely than females to have a bank account.

In this assignment I have concentrated on current accounts and mortgages, but there are many different aspects of competition between banks and building societies, for example the provision of foreign currency and travellers' cheques, insurance cover, opening hours, and personal financial advice.

The future

I think that I have found evidence of a growing war between banks and building societies. Perhaps we will see much longer opening hours, including Sunday opening. To match the piggy-banks and other treats being offered to children, there might be 'adult' gimmicks such as free wine glasses (like at petrol stations) or bingo cards. At least one bank belongs to the 'Air Miles' scheme, allowing customers to collect coupons which they can swop for air tickets. For many years, banks resisted abolishing bank charges and paying interest on their current accounts, and these gimmicks can be seen as a tactic to delay having to do these things. The trigger for the banks' rush to offer more attractive current accounts has been the success of building societies in winning new customers, either with card-based current accounts, or (in the case of Abbey National and Nationwide Anglia) with cheque-book based accounts). These trends will offer more choice to the consumer. The competition is probably a healthy sign: the commercial banks have been forcibly reminded, in the words of one TV advertisement, that it is our money that they are dealing with.

We will discuss the quality of Sally's assignment later in this chapter. First we introduce you to our second model student, Matthew, who is a Fifth Form student at the Newton Comprehensive School, Harlowsden. His Economics teacher is Mrs. Marshall.

UNIT 3 — MATTHEW'S ASSIGNMENT

3.1 Stage 1: Choosing a Topic

Matthew began working on his assessed assignments roughly half-way through the Fourth Year. He was anxious to get started on his GCSE coursework, as he did not want too many assignment deadlines to be concentrated together towards the end of the course. For his first assignment, he required a topic which is usually taught at quite an early stage in an economics course. This was the main factor in Matthew's choice of 'The Growth of Firms and Economies of Scale'.

3.2 Stage 2: Choosing a Title

Mrs. Marshall advised Matthew that 'The Growth of Firms' is a very broad topic, and that a narrower title would be more manageable. The title which they eventually agreed upon was 'A Study of the Economic Factors Influencing the Growth of Selected Firms in the Harlowsden Area'.

3.3 Stage 3: Taking Aim

Even with this specific title, the assignment needed a clearer aim. Matthew decided that he would aim to answer the following question:

For what reasons have firms expanded in Harlowsden in recent years?

3.4 Stage 4: Planning

Matthew decided that it was impossible to survey all the firms in Harlowsden. He would therefore select one, or perhaps two, firms and undertake a 'case study' approach, in the hope that some patterns would emerge which might apply to most firms.

3.5 Stage 5: Preparation

Mrs. Marshall is very keen on the idea that an Economics assignment should test a piece of Economic theory, and encouraged Matthew to build this idea into his coursework. With this in mind, Matthew mapped out the following structure for his assignment:

MATTHEW'S SYNOPSIS

- *Aim*: to discover the factors influencing local firms in their decisions to expand.
- *Methodology*: to put forward the relevant economic theory and to use fieldwork to assess the extent the economic theory is appropriate.
- *Theory being tested*: standard textbook treatment of a) factors influencing investment, b) internal economies of scale.
- *Fieldwork*: case studies of two local firms with a reputation for expansion and growth.
- *Conclusions*.

3.6 Stage 6: Gathering Information

Mrs. Marshall arranged a class visit to a local factory, Stirling Hydraulics, which manufactures brake components for the motor industry. While there, Matthew made notes on what the class was shown, and made a point of asking questions about factors influencing the growth of the firm.

Having studied a mass production factory in the secondary sector Matthew decided to look also at an expanding business in the tertiary sector. He was able to link this with work experience at a local hotel. The Greenacres Hotel had recently undergone substantial rebuilding, and this would give Matthew an opportunity to ask the proprietors about their reasons for investing expansion.

The information which Matthew picked up on these visits gave him some ideas for a very brief questionnaire which he posted to the managers of around a dozen other firms in the area, with a stamped addressed envelope for their reply. Six of these firms took the trouble to return the completed questionnaire.

3.7 Stage 7: Using Information

Matthew found that some of his results were quite surprising. For example, some industrialists were denying that interest rates were significantly affecting their decisions to invest and expand, while economics textbooks seem to suggest that interest rates are an important consideration. Mrs. Marshall said that it seemed that investment decisions might be 'inelastic' with respect to interest rate changes, and suggested that Matthew might like to consider the effect that high interest rates would have on the costs of production of the firms investigated.

3.8 Stage 8: Writing and Presentation

In order to help her students with writing and presentation, Mrs. Marshall gives them a 'Checklist' which they can use during the writing of assignments to ensure that everything important is included and set out properly:

```
                    Mrs. Marshall's Checklist
I will give you one copy of this checklist for each of your economics
assignments. Be sure to make a note on the checklist of the date on
which the assignment is handed to me for marking; I will sign the
checklist to acknowledge receipt of your assignment.

Do NOT hand in any assignment for marking unless ALL these items have
been checked. This will help to ensure that your coursework is
properly organised, attractively presented, and is something which the
examiner will want to look at. Remember that examiners might have to
read hundreds of assignments. Scruffy binders, sloppy presentation,
poor organisation, crumpled pages, and illegible handwriting are the
enemies of all teachers and examiners.
                                                         J.K.Marshall
............................................................................
                              CHECKLIST
Your name         ........................................
Assignment title    ......................................
Date submitted       .....................................
Teacher's signature    ...................................

Does the front cover of your coursework show each
of the following details?                                    TICK
                                                             .....
Your full name         ...............................:....:
The name of the exam. centre   .......................:....:
The centre number          ...........................:....:
Your candidate number    .............................:....:
The heading "GCSE Economics Coursework"  .............:....:
Assignment title      ................................:....:

At the start of the assignment...
                                                             .....
Is there a title page?       .........................:....:
Is there a 'contents' page?   ........................:....:
Is the purpose of the assignment clearly stated?   ...:....:

Within the assignment...
                                                             .....
Are the pages numbered?     ..........................:....:
Are all pages neat and tidy?   .......................:....:
Is all handwriting legible?   ........................:....:
Are diagrams clear, and labelled?   ..................:....:

At the end of the assignment...
                                                             .....
Have you stated your conclusions?    .................:....:
Is there a bibliography/list of sources?   ...........:....:
Is there a summary of research methods used?    ......:....:
Have you commented on the usefulness of the books /    .....
sources / methods used in your coursework?    ........:....:
Have you signed a declaration?    ....................:....:
If applicable, has any additional                      .....
material been gathered into an 'Appendix'?    ........:....:
............................................................................
```

UNIT 4 — EXTRACTS FROM MATTHEW'S ASSIGNMENT

(1) Title

A Study of the Economic Factors Influencing the Growth of Selected Firms in the Harlowsden Area.

(2) Aims of this assignment

The aim of this assignment is to answer the question:

For what reasons have firms in Harlowsden expanded in recent years?

Methodology

I decided to explore (a) factors influencing investment decisions, (b) internal economies of scale. These concepts are closely related to each other, because investment decisions can cause a firm to expand, and therefore the possibility of benefitting from internal economies of scale might be an additional factor influencing these decisions.

Permission was obtained for my economics class to visit Stirling Hydraulics on the Harlowsden Newtown Business Park. This firm produces brake components for the car industry. There we met Mr. Khan, the production manager. I had an opportunity to ask Mr. Khan about reasons for the firm's expansion in Harlowsden. The interview was tape-recorded, and after a detailed discussion and a full guided tour of the factory, the answers were taken back to school and analysed to compare with economic theory.

I then decided to study a smaller firm. I had already made enquiries with my careers teacher about the possibility of work experience in the locality, and it seemed sensible to tie this in with my Economics coursework if possible. Luckily, she was able to arrange a week's work experience at the Greenacres Hotel, on the outskirts of the Oldtown area of Harlowsden. The proprietor, Mrs. Mackenzie, was very helpful in explaining why she and her husband had decided to expand their business.

I sent a short questionnaire to the managing directors of a selection of firms in the district, and received a few replies.

(3) Economic theory being tested

(a) Factors influencing the investment decisions of firms

Textbooks normally list the following factors:

Interest rates. Economists usually argue that as interest rates rise, the level of investment falls.

For example, a taxi company considering investing £10,000 in a new taxi will estimate the value of future earnings from their investment. They will want these earnings to be higher than the interest that could have been earned by investing £10,000 elsewhere. If interest rates are generally high, then the opportunity cost of buying the taxi is high. The firm is therefore more likely to invest in a taxi if interest rates are low.

If the taxi firm needs to borrow the £10,000 then it seems quite obvious to do this when interest rates are low. Interest rates are the 'price' of investment funds, and are inversely related to the demand for investment. This simply means that as interest rates go down, the demand for investment funds will go up.

* Consumer demand. The greater the demand for consumer goods and services, the greater the demand for the investment goods which are used to produce them. For example, a substantial increase in the demand for ice cream will lead to increased investment by manufacturers in new ice-cream making machinery.

* The price of capital goods. If the purchase price of a new plant and equipment rises faster than the prices at which output can be sold, then investment is discouraged. This is because the demand for producer goods is derived from the demand for consumer goods.

* Expectations or 'business confidence'. As well as reacting to changes in consumer demand, firms also try to estimate the future demand for their products and their confidence in the future can influence their decisions to invest at the present time. 'Business confidence' is not an easy idea to pin down or to measure, but it can be encouraged by such things as expanding markets, a buoyant economy, rising incomes, political stability, government incentives, and low taxes. It can be harmed by things such as rapid inflation, trade restrictions, and bad labour relations. It can be argued, for example, that investment in an industry prone to frequent strike action might be harmed because of a lack of business confidence. It has also been argued that a government with 'go-stop' policies (where consumer spending is at first encouraged and then suddenly discouraged, for example by tax cuts being closely followed by interest rate rises) can harm business confidence by making the future course of the economy less predictable.

* Innovation, enterprise and technology. Public attitudes towards such things as new inventions, new products, and new technology are important influences on investment and expansion. A country is said to be more likely to experience long-term economic growth if its population are willing to innovate, take risks, adopt enterprising attitudes and forgo present consumption in order to increase investment for the future.

(b) Internal economies of scale

Internal economies of scale exist where the long run average costs of production decrease as a firm increases in size. These cost reductions give large firms an advantage over small firms. Economies stem from various sources:

* Technical economies arise because larger firms can afford to by more efficient machines, and can organise themselves to use more efficient production methods.

* Marketing economies arise because it is cheaper to buy in bulk, and larger firms can use large scale marketing techniques such as TV advertising which smaller firms cannot afford.

* Financial economies arise because a larger firm can raise money more easily and can negotiate cheaper loans.

* Managerial economies arise because a larger firm can employ specialist administrative staff.

* Risk-bearing economies arise because a larger firm can sell in a range of markets, and can diversify its products, instead of 'putting all its eggs in one basket' by providing only a single product.

(4) Fieldwork

(a) Class visit to Stirling Hydraulics, Harlowsden

On 7 February 1989 our Economics class travelled to the Harlowsden Newtown Business Park to visit the Stirling Hydraulics factory. We were greeted by Mr S. Khan, the Production Manager and were shown to the conference room where Mr. Khan gave us a brief history of the company.

Mr. Khan explained that Stirling is a multi-national company, with its headquarters in Detroit, USA. In the early 1970s, following Britain's entry into the EEC, the company decided to set up a factory in the UK. Three sites were considered: Newcastle, Wolverhampton and Harlowsden.

CHAPTER THREE EXTRACTS FROM MATTHEW'S ASSIGNMENT

The latter was chosen for a variety of reasons, including its good communications and the availability of government granst. Another consideration was its nearness to the port of Bowness, which enables Stirling to easily export its products. The company has a warehouse and distribution centre at Rotterdam which it uses to supply its continental customers.

In 1987 there were rumours and press reports that Stirling would be closing its Harlowsden plant and centralising all its operations on the continent. Some of my classmates whose parents work at the factory said that Stirling workers were on a 'four-day week' and some were threatened with redundancy. However, later in the same year the company announced a major investment programme in Harlowsden, safeguarding the existing 500 jobs and promising another 250. This is what I was particularly interested in, and Mr. Khan kindly allowed me to tape-record an interview on the reasons for expansion.

I asked him to name the five most important economic factors for the expansion of Stirling at Harlowsden in rank order, and this is the answer he gave:

1 Access to markets in Europe. During the 1987 general election all major parties were committed to staying in the EEC and this convinced Stirling management in Detroit that they should stay at Harlowsden. At about the same time, contracts were awarded to build the Channel Tunnel, and companies were becoming more aware of the importance of the 'single market' to be introduced by the EEC in 1992.
2 The promise of government grants. These were available, because Harlowsden qualified as an Assisted Area.
3 The skilled workforce at Harlowsden, into which the company had invested a lot of money in the past by way of training.
4 Skilled management. At Harlowsden the company had managers who knew the business and knew their markets; investing at Harlowsden therefore built upon this expertise which might have been lost if the firm had moved elsewhere.
5 Local support. To expand at Harlowsden the company, the company would require planning permission to extend its factory. Stirling was confident that the local authority would support the scheme.

When I asked Mr. Khan if he could think of any more factors influencing the decision he said that there might have been other considerations, but whatever they were he dismissed them as 'unimportant'.

During our guided tour of the factory, our attention was drawn to some internal economies. We were shown a new machine which had been very expensive to install, but which does the work of twelve of the old machines and in the long run will cut average costs immensely. I asked Mr. Khan why he did not mention this new technology as one of his five influences on expansion, and he replied that technical changes such as this would have been necessary anyway, wherever the company had expanded. He had given me a list of particular reasons why Stirling had expanded at Harlowsden.

I asked Mr. Khan whether interest rates were an important factor influencing the expansion of Stirling. He replied that the firm had to take a long term view: if the company had confidence in the future of the Harlowsden plant, then they would invest. Mr. Khan's reply was rather surprising because he was quite insistent that interest rates had 'no effect'. He said that high interest rates were a 'short-term nuisance' and were annoying because they caused companies to pay more for doing something which they had to do anyway, which was to expand in order to compete internationally and capture markets. He did say, however, that if interest rates rose to very high levels there might come a time when the firm might consider cutting back on its investment at Harlowsden, but he did not think that this point was likely to be reached.

After some thought, however, Mr. Khan added that he would welcome lower interest rates if this would help to reduce the exchange rate of the pound. A company which exports a high proportion of its output, Stirling does not like the pound to be over-valued on currency markets, as this makes our exports dearer abroad. Mr. Khan also mentioned that recent cuts in corporation tax had given a boost to the investment.

On returning to school, and analysing Mr. Khan's comments, I found that his reasons for expansion were not quite what my textbooks had led me to expect, especially his strong denial of the importance of interest rates. This contradicts the recent strong complaints from the Confederation of British Industry (CBI) about high interest rates. One firm is, of course, a very small sample and so I decided to investigate further, during a period of work experience.

(b) Work experience

During the last week of February 1989, I did work experience at Greenacres Hotel, which is situated on the outskirts of the Oldtown area of Harlowsden. This business was originally a public house, but when the new by-pass was built the licensee, Mrs. Mackenzie, realised that there would be an increase in passing trade, due to the fact that a new access roundabout would be very close by. With a well-designed illuminated hoarding she could attract passing motorists off the by-pass.

She had also noticed a change in public tastes away from the old-fashioned pub, and in favour of a wider range of eating-out facilities. Motorists, in particular, were demanding an atmosphere less geared towards the selling of alcohol. She contacted the brewery for their support in obtaining plannning permission and providing part of the investment funds for turning the pub into an hotel with restaurant and bars. Although the brewery would provide some backing, Mrs. Mackenzie and her husband also had to provide some finance. In order to do this she had to approach her bank manager for a business loan.

During my week at the hotel I worked in most sections from reception to the kitchens (although being under 18 I was not allowed to work behind the bar) and I noticed the business was brisk. I asked Mrs. Mackenzie the same question I had asked Mr. Khan: to list five factors which had influenced her decision to expand, in order of importance. She listed the following:

1 Changed market conditions following the building of the by-pass, and increased public demand for 'eating out' and tourist facilities.
2 The availability of a loan from the bank.
3 Confidence in the future of the business (without this there would have been no support for the brewery).
4 The promise of a grant from the English Tourist Board.
5 The cost of rebuilding the premises, and the availability of suitable tenders at the right price from local building firms.

I asked Mrs. Mackenzie whether interest rates came into number 2, and she explained that at the time, the availability of the loan seemed more important than the interest rate, although she felt fortunate that at the time interest rates were not too high. I asked whether the higher interest rates were experiencing recently would have stopped her expansion, but she wasn't sure.

(c) Questionnaire

In the light of what I had learned so far I designed a simple questionnaire, which I sent to the managing directors of a dozen local companies. I explained that I was a student undertaking a GCSE project, and asked the respondent (the person replying to the questionnaire) to list the five most important reasons for recent investment decisions by the company, in order of priority. This questionnaire was therefore 'open ended' in the sense that the respondents were asked to name their own five influences, not to choose from a list provided by myself. I thought that it would be interesting to compare their answers with the reasons for expansion suggested in Economics textbooks. I also asked the respondent to tick 'yes' or 'no' to a specific question: Would increased interest rates be a serious barrier to further investment? I put this question at the end of the questionnaire, so that it would not influence the respondents in their initial choice of five factors. I enclosed a stamped addressed envelope, and tried to choose a mixture of small medium and large firms. Six of the managing directors were kind enough to reply, and their answers are summarised in Figure 3.5, together with the results of my fieldwork, making a sample of eight altogether.

The bar chart shows the main items mentioned by business people when asked to list five factors influencing recent business expansion. Obviously, respondents did not all use exactly the same words to describe their factors, so I have tried to group similar replies together. The box in Figure 3.5 shows how respondents then replied to a specific question about interest rates. Note that although only two respondents volunteered interest rates as an influence, three respondents went on to answer 'yes' to my question on interest rates.

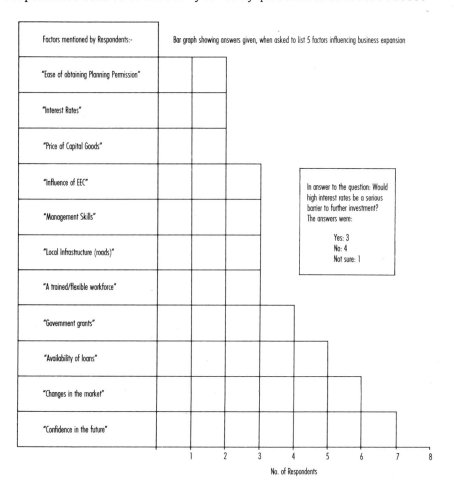

Fig 3.5

(5) Conclusions

My survey was clearly limited in its coverage, and I would have preferred to have had a larger sample. However, it seems to me that there are many factors which influence the decisions of the firms to invest and expand. At some times some of these factors seem more important than other times. This is not always made clear in Economics textbooks.

In the case of Stirling Hydraulics, the decision on whether to expand was made at Detroit in response to European market conditions, and the next important decision, as it affected Mr. Khan and his workforce, was the question of where to expand. Mr. Khan's list therefore consisted mainly of locational factors favouring Harlowsden over other places in Europe.

In the case of Greenacres, again it was a case of 'changed market conditions' (including the effects of the new road layout) which provided the initial reason for expansion, but the question of 'where' did not come into it: it was always clear that expansion would take place on the present site. Now that the business is expanding, the proprietors will no doubt begin to notice the benefits of internal economies of scale.

My enquiries left me wondering whether some Economics textbooks might be putting too much stress on the importance of interest rates. It is possible that, in economic terminology, the demand for funds for investment purposes is fairly inelastic with respect to interest rate changes. An expanding market seems to be much more important, as it gives industrialists confidence in their ability to sell more goods and services and possibly enables them to benefit from internal economies of scale, so that their profits increase.

It is significant that the two respondents who answered 'yes' to my question on interest rates came from relatively small firms, and Mrs. Mackenzie, who when pressed agreed that interest rates might be important belonged to a smaller enterprise than Mr. Khan who wanted to deny their importance altogether.

It is therefore possible that high interest rates are more damaging to small firms than large firms. One possible reason is that smaller firms often have 'cash-flow' problems (they can run short of the cash that they need to meet day-to-day expenses) and these can be made worse by unpredictable interest rates.

If my argument is true it would support the view that there are important economies of scale to be gained when a firm expands. In other words, high interest rates might be something of a deterrent to the expansion of a small firm, but if a firm does manage to expand, then economies of scale help to act as a shield againsta the effect of high interest rates on the firm's costs.

In general, expansion decisions depend very much on the type of firm and industry, as different firms have different needs and preferences. It is therefore necessary to have careful planning and deliberation to discover whether expansion and growth is desirable.

CHAPTER 4

OUTLINE OF MARKING SCHEMES

Before we discuss the quality of the work done by Sally and Matthew, we must consider the *marking schemes* which are used in order to assess coursework.

UNIT 1 ASSESSMENT CRITERIA

When coursework is used for assessment, there comes a time when your friendly, familiar teacher must put on a different cap and become your *examiner*. Do not be afraid! He or she will not become unfriendly or distant overnight. One of the main reasons for having coursework is the fact that the person best qualified to assess your work in economics is none other than your Economics teacher; this is for the simple reason that he or she has worked with you for two years and knows better than anyone else how well you have worked.

Naturally, it is necessary for the Examination Boards and Groups to ensure that teachers use constant standards (criteria). In order to achieve this, your teacher's marking of your coursework will be *moderated*, either by other teachers ('consensus' moderation) or by a specially appointed moderator ('external' moderation). If, during moderation, your teacher is judged to be marking too harshly or generously, his or her marks will be 'scaled' upwards or downwards as appropriate.

Table 4.1 shows how teachers are instructed to mark your coursework. The final column shows how marks are 'weighted' to achieve the percentage of marks for coursework laid down in the syllabus. For example, an SEG candidate receiving full marks for coursework (25 marks per piece) would receive $2 \times 25 \times 2/5 = 20\%$ of the total marks for the examination. Another candidate earning 15 marks on one piece and 20 on the other would receive $(15 + 20) \times 2/5 = 14\%$.

Exam	Criteria	Max. marks	Weighting
LEAG	Treatment	7	
	Range of material	5	
	Analysis	7	$3 \times 33 \times \dfrac{1}{4} = 25$
	Presentation	7	
	Economic ideas	7	
		33	
MEG	Collection and presentation of relevant data	15	$3 \times 40 \times \dfrac{5}{24} = 25$
	Analysis, interpretation and evaluation of data collected	25	
		40	
NEA	Recognise, select and present relevant data	15	$1 \times 40 \times \dfrac{3}{4}$
	Analyse and interpret the data and apply it in an appropriate way	15	or
	Make reasoned judgements based on economic principles	10	$2 \times 40 \times \dfrac{3}{8}$
		40	or
			$3 \times 40 \times \dfrac{3}{12}$
			$= 30$

NISEC	Research	4	$1 \times 20 = 20$
	Analysis	6	
	Evaluation	6	
	Presentation	4	
		20	
SEG	Information	4	$2 \times 25 \times \frac{2}{5} = 20$
	Analysis	8	
	Evaluation	8	
	Presentation	5	
		25	
WJEC Fieldwork	Understanding and communication	5	$1 \times 20 = 20$
	Analysis and interpretation	5	
	Evaluation	5	
	Autonomy	5	
		20	
Project	Understanding and communication	3	$2 \times 10 = 20$
	Analysis and interpretation	3	
	Evaluation	4	
		10	

Table 4.1
Main Marking Criteria

UNIT 2 — MARKING SCHEMES

When marking your work, your teacher will use a *marking scheme* laid down by the board or group. Economics marking schemes consist of 'criteria' which are closely related to the 'assessment objectives' laid down in your syllabus and the skills which we have discussed in Chapter 1. These criteria are shown in Table 4.1, together with the maximum marks available for each one. The criteria are further broken down into 'Levels of Response' to show more exactly how marks are awarded within each criterion. These Levels of Response are shown in Table 4.2.

The Levels of Response can be thought of in the same way as 'distance badges', which are awarded to young people learning to swim. If you cannot swim at all, you have no badge; the more lengths you can swim, the more badges you get. After a certain level, you can no longer win badges simply on distance: you have to improve your stroke as well. The same thing happens with Levels of Response; to achieve the higher levels you must demonstrate *quality* as well as *quantity*.

Eventually, it is planned that all GCSE syllabuses will be 'criterion referenced', which means that candidates in any subject will know exactly what they have to do to achieve any grade. Unfortunately, the 'state-of-the-art' of criterion referencing is a long way short of this ideal at present, and the degree of assistance given to teachers by the boards varies greatly. One group simply asks your teacher to use two criteria when awarding marks. At the other extreme, another group lays down five 'marking criteria', with three or four levels within each criterion.

You will notice from the tables that the way in which 'criteria' and 'levels' are described varies considerably from board to board. Some of the language used in the tables might seem strange and difficult to you. Do not worry; in chapter 5 we have included a 'self-assessment' mark scheme, to help you to judge whether your own work is likely to achieve most of the marks available.

Exam Group	*Marks*
LEAG	
Treatment	
Provides a brief outline only.	1
Gives a straightforward treatment of the subject.	2–4
Shows a thorough knowledge of the chosen theme.	5–6
Demonstrates an understanding of the interdependence of the subject matter of economics.	7

Range of material

Relies exclusively on textual material in the assignment.	1
Offers some source material in the assignment.	2
Uses a variety of source material in the assignment.	3–4
Uses a wide range of appropriate and relevant source material.	5

Analysis of material

Arranges material to present a descriptive account.	1
Offers comments on textual material.	2–4
Draws conclusions from the evidence presented.	5
Uses a wide range of material which shows clear evidence of logical arrangement, resulting in interpretative conclusions.	6–7

Presentation

Shows some evidence of concern for an orderly arrangement.	1–3
Shows clear evidence of care in arrangement and presentation.	4–5
Demonstrates a logical and orderly presentation.	6
Demonstrates a high standard of orderly presentation.	7

Economic ideas

Demonstrates some knowledge of basic economic concepts.	1–3
Shows a thorough knowledge of basic economic concepts.	4
Applies economic concepts in a relevant and appropriate manner throughout the assignment.	5–7

Max. total marks = 33

MEG

Collection & presentation of relevant data

No relevant information collected or presented.	0
Attempt made to gather information of little relevance from limited sources. Some limited understanding of appropriate presentation methods but very poorly presented.	1–3
Attempt made to gather some relevant information from wider sources. Better understanding of appropriate presentation with some variation but poorly applied.	4–6
Information collected from many sources using a variety of techniques and is presented using some different and appropriate methods.	7–9
Information collected is relevant to the topic using appropriate methods with some evidence of original research. Clear presentation with evidence of attempts to convert data into different and appropriate forms of communication.	10–12
Information collected is clearly linked to the topic set and throughout appropriate methods of collection have been well applied. There is evidence of considerable research and detailed understanding of the data used. Materials are fully and clearly explained and a complete range of presentation skills used.	13–15

Analysis, interpretation and evaluation of data collected

No relevant analysis, interpretation or evaluation of the topic.	0
Attempt to organise material into parts and build argument, but tendency to make unsupported generalisations. A lack of economic ideas or original conclusion.	1–5

Some attempt to use material in a logical manner with a limited application of economic ideas. Evaluation based largely upon the acceptance of others' opinions with limited criticism.	6–10
Work planned in a logical manner with an attempt to break down material in a reasonably clear and sensible way. Some applications of economic ideas and techniques demonstrating some ability to use reasoned logical arguments applied to the topic.	11–15
Able to break down material in a clear and logical manner and highlight main points. Economic ideas generally applied well to the topic. Shows some ability to examine critically argument and statements of opinion and understanding in applying judgements and recommendations to the topic.	16–20
Evidence of original and clear analysis of the topic with relevant and accurate use of economic ideas. Shows real ability to examine critically arguments and opinion. Ability to distinguish between evidence and value judgement demonstrating originality and imagination in solutions and conclusions.	21–25

Max. total marks = 40

NEA

Recognise, select and present relevant data

A small amount of data collected.	1–3
Some evidence of an attempt to meet the research aims and to present the data collected.	4–7
A clear attempt has been made to achieve the relevant research aims with collection of some relevant data, reasonably presented.	8–11
Clear evidence that candidates know what they are looking for, why they are looking for it and how to select suitable data. Data used is appropriate for research aims. Data methodically collected and well organised. A variety of presentation techniques.	12–15

Analyse and interpret the data and apply it in an appropriate way.

No evidence of any attempt to analyse data.	0
A little analysis. Evidence of a limited attempt to interpret or apply data.	1–3
Some attempt made at analysis but weaknesses in candidate's ability to analyse and apply material.	4–7
Competent analysis and interpretation of data but lack of depth in candidate's ability to apply data to research aims.	8–11
Clear powers of analysis shown. Accurate interpretation of material collected. Data applied in manner appropriate to aims of research.	12–15

Make reasoned judgements based on economic principles

No evidence of any attempt to make reasoned judgements.	0
A little evidence of an attempt to form conclusions or to refer to economic principles.	1–2
Some attempt to use economic principles to support conclusions.	3–6
Excellent application of economic principles. Clear evidence of ability to make reasoned judgements.	7–10

Max. total marks = 40

NISEC

Method of research and relevant information collected

No relevant information collected or presented.	0
Attempt made to gather information from limited resources and of limited relevance.	1

Evidence of knowledge of information required with some attempt to use appropriate methods to gather this. Some background material obtained.	2
More relevant information collected using appropriate methods with some evidence of background research applicable to the problem.	3
Information gathering is very clearly linked to the problem in question. Appropriate methods of research used and relevant information collected.	4

Analysis

No relevant analysis of the material.	0
Some attempt to break down material into various parts. A limited attempt to select and apply information to the problem with some limited use of economic ideas, techniques, etc.	1–2
Able to break down material in a reasonably clear and logical fashion. Work is well planned so that some of the salient features are highlighted. Generally able to apply these ideas and techniques to the problem or situation.	3–4
Evidence of original and clear analysis of the problem with relevant and accurate use of economic ideas, techniques, etc.	5–6

Evaluation

No production of any results or of any conclusions.	0
Limited attempt at building an argument but tendency to be unsupported or based on generalisation. Acceptance and use of others' opinion with limited criticism. Limited attempt to distinguish between fact and opinion and to reach conclusions.	1–2
Shows some ability to build logical arguments; use judgements; distinguish between statements of fact and statements of opinion; reach conclusions.	3–4
Shows a real ability to examine arguments and statements. Can differentiate between a well supported argument and a statement of opinion. Clear evidence of ability to make reasoned judgements and reach conclusions.	5–6

Presentation

No appropriate format.	0
An attempt made to use an appropriate range of presentation techniques and to convert information into other forms of communication where appropriate.	1–2
Materials fully and clearly explained and a good range of presentation techniques demonstrated.	3–4

Max. total marks = 20

SEG

Information

No relevant information collected or presented.	0
Attempt made to gather information from limited sources and of limited relevance.	1
Evidence of knowledge of information required with some attempt to use appropriate techniques to gather this. Some background material obtained but not specifically applied to the problem.	2
Information collected is relevant to problem using appropriate methods with some evidence of background research being applied to the problem.	3
Information gathering is very clearly linked to the problem in question. Appropriate methods of collection, well applied. Evidence of considerable research and understanding of information used.	4

Analysis

No relevant analysis of the material.	0

Some effort to break down material into various parts, but tendency to make unsupported generalisations. A little attempt to apply information to the problem under analysis with some limited use of economic ideas, techniques, etc.	1–2
Some attempt to break down material in a fairly clear and logical fashion. Reasonable attempt to plan work in a logical manner. Some application of economic ideas, techniques etc. to problem or situation.	3–4
Able to break down material in a reasonably clear and logical fashion. Work is well planned so that some of the salient features are highlighted. Generally able to apply these ideas and techniques to problem or situation.	5–6
Evidence of original and clear analysis of problem with relevant and accurate use of economic ideas, techniques etc.	7–8

Evaluation

No production of any results or of any conclusions.	0
Some attempt at building an argument but tendency to be unsupported or based on generalisation. Presents solutions but these tend to be based on the uncritical use of others' work.	1–2
Acceptance and use of others' opinions with limited criticism. Some attempt to make comments and arrive at conclusions, judgements or recommendations, but mostly second-hand.	3–4
Shows some ability to examine critically argument and statements to show differing opinions. Shows some perception and understanding in applying judgements and recommendations to the problem.	5–6
Shows a real ability to examine critically arguments and statements. Can differentiate between a well supported argument and a statement of opinion. Is able to make judgements about the accuracy and reliability of solutions to problems. Shows originality and imagination in solutions and conclusions.	7–8

Presentation

No understanding of an appropriate format.	0
Some very limited understanding of an appropriate format but not well applied.	1
An attempt made to apply and convert information into other forms of communication where appropriate.	2–3
Materials fully and clearly explained and a good range of presentation skills demonstrated. Full use of appropriate economic terminology.	4–5

Max. total marks = 25

WJEC

	Project	Fieldwork
Understanding and communication		
An inadequate attempt to achieve the aims of the assignment; limited organisation and presentation of research findings.	0 or 1	0 or 1
A positive attempt has been made to achieve the aims of the assignment, but both collection and presentation of the data are limited in scope; some facility to organise data in a rudimentary manner only.	2	2 or 3
An ability to recognise, collect and present relevant data and to use and comment on information, well presented in a variety of forms, in an accurate and logical manner.	3	4 or 5
Analysis and interpretation		
An inadequate demonstration of analytical and interpretative skills; limited attempt to apply data.	0 or 1	0 or 1
A competent analysis and interpretation of data, but lacks direct correlation with the assignment's aims.	2	2 or 3

	Project	Fieldwork
An ability to select, analyse, interpret and organise complex information demonstrated; data interpreted accurately and analysed logically in a manner appropriate to the aims of the assignment.	3	4 or 5

Evaluation based on economic principles

	Project	Fieldwork
Application and judgemental skills not greatly developed; only a tenuous link between economic concepts and aims of assignment.	0 or 1	0 or 1
An ability to engage in simple interpretations based on some familiarity with central concepts and ideas.	2	2 or 3
An ability to apply appropriate terminology, concepts and elementary theory, and to evaluate and make reasoned judgements in an accurate and logical manner, supporting the assignment's aims.	3 or 4	4 or 5

Autonomy (Fieldwork only)

	Project	Fieldwork
Insufficient initiative and cooperation to complete the task without continuing support throughout the process of investigation and reporting.	–	0 or 1
An ability to originate fieldwork successfully, but requires support at various crucial stages in the study in order to complete the process successfully.	–	2 or 3
An ability to initiate successful negotiations with the teacher, consultant and others; develop positive attitudes towards problem-solving in co-operation with others and to complete the set task successfully.	–	4 or 5
Max. total marks =	10	20

CHAPTER 5

ASSESSING YOUR OWN COURSEWORK

If you wish to monitor your *own* progress, or to assess your assignments when they are completed, you can try using the appropriate mark scheme for your syllabus, selected from those in Chapter 4. We apply some of them to the sample assignments presented in Chapter 6.

Alternatively, you can use our 'self-assessment' schedule, which is presented below, or you might wish to use both our scheme *and* your Board's official one, as a double-check. It is always worth getting a second (or third) opinion of the quality of your work from parents or friends, and of course you should never be afraid to ask for your teacher's opinion of how you are progressing.

UNIT 1 SELF-ASSESSMENT MARK SCHEME

▸ When marking your coursework your teacher will be looking for *evidence* of what you *know, understand,* and *can do.*
▸ *You* must provide the evidence *in your coursework* to prove to the examiner that you have the skills that he or she is looking for.
▸ First, to make sure that your *presentation* is of a good standard, look at the *checklist* on page 00, and make sure that you can complete it for your coursework assignment.
▸ Then ask yourself the following questions, and answer them truthfully by ticking either:

column 0 = No/don't know;
column 1 = Possibly;
column 2 = Probably;
column 3 = Definitely.

In your coursework, have you . . .

	0	1	2	3

a) demonstrated your ability to use the *language* of economics?
b) shown that you have a good *understanding* of economic concepts?
c) given clear and accurate *definitions* of important terms?
d) *distinguished* clearly between different economic concepts?
e) drawn on *examples* which show that you can relate economic concepts to the real world?
f) *used* economic theory and applied it to your project title?
g) *selected* facts and/or theories, and decided which are relevant?
h) shown that you can *separate* facts from opinions?
i) *presented* your findings in interesting ways?
j) drawn *conclusions*?
k) given two sides of an *argument*?
l) *brought together* different strands of economics from different parts of the syllabus?
m) tackled your work in a *logical* way?
n) shown some *originality*?
o) *evaluated* your work?

Having been honest and truthful with yourself, you can award yourself 3 marks for each tick in column 3, 2 marks for each tick in column 2, and 1 mark for each tick in column 1. Award yourself a further 5 marks if you can fully complete the presentation checklist on page 44.

Then find your total, and you have a mark out of 50. Double this to find your percentage.
WARNING: This cannot be guaranteed to give the same mark as will be awarded to your coursework by your examiners. However it does give you some indication of how well you are doing, and will help you see where you can try to improve your coursework before it is submitted.

You should certainly aim to get as many ticks as you can in Column 3, *especially* for categories a) to j).

If you have several ticks in column 0, then this indicates that you are not sure of what it is that your coursework is achieving, and you should seek advice from your teacher on ways of improving your assignment before submission.

UNIT 2 — ASSESSMENT OF SALLY AND MATTHEW'S ASSIGNMENTS

Using this mark scheme to assess the model answers in Chapter 3, we hope you will agree that both Sally and Matthew would deserve very high marks. They do well under most of the categories listed above, although Sally perhaps scores more highly than Matthew in terms of category i), because she has presented data in a greater variety of interesting ways. Matthew, however, scores highly under f), g) and l) for using theory to gain insights into the way his local economy works. Both do well under m), o) and j) for their logical approach, and for their good evaluation and sensible conclusions.

CHAPTER 6

SAMPLE ASSIGNMENTS WITH EXAMINER COMMENTS

In this chapter we show you some samples of coursework written by students. We have put some examiner comments in the margins to guide you as you read the sample material. Following each assignment are some general comments assessing the piece of coursework as a whole. Our intention in making these comments is not to discourage or to find fault, but to suggest ways in which candidates could obtain some extra marks.

Rather than present these assignments to you in handwritten form, we have had them printed. If *you* wish to use a typewriter or word-processor to prepare your assignments you must check with your teacher to see whether this is permitted. At the time of writing this book, the Boards and Groups were considering their policy on this matter. Generally, examiners say that it should make no difference to your marks whether your coursework is handwritten, typed or word-processed. So our advice is to use 'technology' only if you genuinely find it more convenient than writing in longhand, and if the regulations allow it. Here and there in the following samples we have made some minor changes for the purposes of publication: for instance, we have re-drawn diagrams where necessary for the printer, and corrected any spelling mistakes together with the more obvious grammatical errors. In other respects, these assignments are the work of students like yourself. In order to avoid any possible embarrassment we refer to the candidates by pen-names.

UNIT 1   KEVIN'S ASSIGNMENT: THE PRICE OF SECOND-HAND CARS

The Price of Second Hand Cars

Aim

I wish to answer the question: what are the main factors which determine the price of a second-hand car? I will try to identify, list and describe these factors. I also have an hypothesis that smaller cars lose their value over a given period more slowly than larger cars. I will try to support this claim through notes and diagrams in the following pages.

Introduction

Using economic principles I will try to justify my claim and complete the project by achieving a comprehensive survey of local car prices, and a description of the types of advertiser and what they aim to achieve through selling their car.

I will collect my statistics from local garages, newspapers and car sales magazines.

The three types of seller that I will write about and compare are:

1   The private seller.
2   Sellers using an auction.
3   Garages.

These are the sources of second-hand cars which determine their supply on the market.

> 'Factors which influence demand' are well covered here, but 'factors which influence supply' are not. Only the *source* of supply are described. You might have mentioned, for example, the massive sale of new cars in August when, in Britain, the registration mark of vehicles changes

CHAPTER SIX KEVIN'S ASSIGNMENT: THE PRICE OF SECOND-HAND CARS

On the demand side the main influences that I will examine are:

1. Model of car, and the price of different models.
2. Age of car.
3. Mileage.
4. Condition of car.
5. Colour.
6. Extras.
7. Terms of repayment.
8. Prestige.
9. Cost of living in an area.
10. Warranty and MOT.
11. Speed and insurance group.
12. Number of previous owners.
13. Whether a car is British.

Types of seller

1 Private seller

This is a member of the public who wishes to sell his or her car. The greater the audience he or she can reach through an advertisement the greater the probability that the car will be sold. Therefore a good way to sell a relatively cheap car is to put an advert in the local newspaper. An example of what is offered is shown in Figure 6.1. Such an advert is of relatively little cost, especially when a car is worth, say, £5,000. Most private sellers are not out to make a profit. Usually they wish to sell their old car in order to purchase a newer one. This is one reason why it is usually cheaper to buy privately rather than from a garage.

The private seller usually needs to sell the car as quickly as possible. To do this the private seller sets a competitive price that enables a quick sale. Often private sellers are inexperienced at selling and may fail to do justice to the car, e.g. by giving it a cheaper price than a garage salesman would.

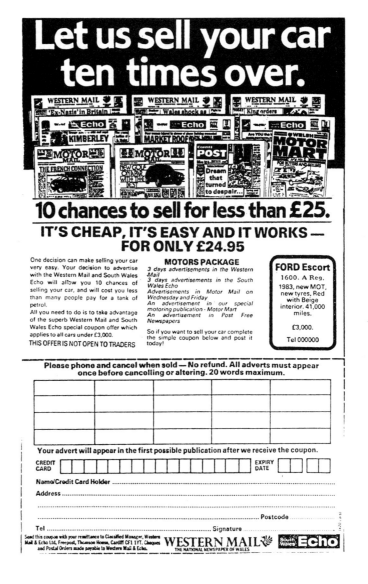

Fig 6.1

The points that are emphasised by private sellers in their adverts are:

   i) The model of the car.
  ii) Age/mileage.
 iii) Colour.
  iv) Condition.
   v) Number of months before next MOT.
  vi) The asking price, often accompanied by the letters 'o.n.o.' (meaning 'or nearest offer'), an invitation to the buyer to 'haggle' over the price.

The important drawback of buying a car privately is that there is no warranty or guarantee after purchase. Therefore buyers like to see an MOT (Ministry of Transport) certificate which should show the car to be roadworthy.

The number of private sellers exceeds the number of garages that advertise in the paper. They are usually contacted by the potential customers over the phone. Fig 6.1 is a form used by private sellers advertising in the Western mail (a daily morning paper, with a circulation throughout Wales) and South Wales Echo (an evening paper covering the South Wales region). The offer also includes an advert in two special motor-sales papers and in a 'freesheet', the Cardiff Post. This seems like a very attractive package, reaching a large number of readers at an economic cost.

2 Auctions

Although this type of selling is not generally well known it is important in the trade, and it advertises to the public in the papers (Fig 6.2). Motor auctions are also sometimes advertised using 'hotspots' on regional commercial television. These are relatively inexpensive announcements by a 'voice-over' with a still picture. I interviewed the owner of the South Wales Motor Auction in Bridgend:

Fig 6.2

Q Do you sell your cars at your car auction by selling to the highest bidder?
A Yes.

Q Do you have a reserve price put on any models?
A Yes, the owner of the car puts a reserve price on the car before the auction.

Q Do you sell any foreign cars? What proportion of all cars sold are foreign?
A Yes, we do sell foreign cars. It depends, but usually about 20% of the cars we sell are foreign.

Q How many cars on average do you sell at an auction per week?
A It depends, but usually 65 to 70 cars a week.

Q Do you sell many prestige cars?
A Not a lot. We sold two Jaguars last week. Right now we don't have any Porsches or Rolls Royces, but we do have a Mercedes to auction this week. We prefer to sell a larger volume of cars at lower prices.

Q Do you sell any commercial vehicles?
A Yes, we have a commercial vehicle sale on once a month. We believe that the prices of the vans and trucks sold at our auctions are very competitive.

CHAPTER SIX KEVIN'S ASSIGNMENT: THE PRICE OF SECOND-HAND CARS

3 Garages

Garages are often integrated with filling stations. Sometimes there are two firms on one site: the petrol company rents the forecourt to a car dealer. Garages get cars from a manufacturer, or from buyers 'trading-in', or from auctions. Some salesmen scour the newspapers for good cheap cars onto which they add a 'mark-up', re-selling the same vehicle at a higher price.

Large garages enjoy economies of scale compared with smaller garages. They sell so many cars that they only need to make a slight profit on each one. They can lower their prices and sell more than smaller competing garages. There is a lot of competition, and garages have many adverts in the newspapers to try to reach a larger audience than their rivals.

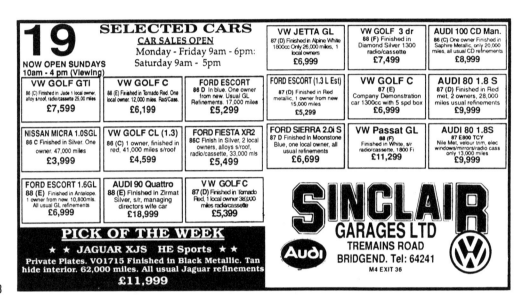

Fig 6.3

Some garages specialise in a certain type of car. Many have a dealership agreement, so they sell the new cars of only one manufacturer, but they normally sell a variety of makes of second-hand car. Figure 6.3 shows an advertisement from a local weekly paper, the Glamorgan Gazette. These models are in the higher price range.

An important advantage dealers have over private sellers and auctions is that they can offer a guarantee on most of their cars. This has an effect on buyers, and influences them to be willing to pay a higher price.

> You could consider whether depreciation by *time* is more important than depreciation by *condition*.

In the newspapers which I surveyed (The South Wales Echo, Western Mail and Glamorgan Gazette) garages take up the majority of vehicle selling space with large eye-catching advertisements. In their adverts they usually comment on the good aspects of the cars they are selling, and naturally any bad aspects are not mentioned. Basically, though, a customer on one visit to a dealer has a large selection of cars to view. This is another reason why garages are so competitive with private sellers.

The factors that influence the demand for a car

> A good use of theory

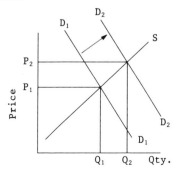

Fig 6.4

1 The model of car the price of the model

Obviously, today's new car is tomorrow's second-hand car. When viewed from the

> **Well done! Relating theory to experience**

angle of the buyer, new cars and second-hand cars are substitutes for each other. An increase in the price of new cars will shift the demand curve for second-hand cars to the right, and increase their price. In Figure 6.4 the supply curve for second-hand cars is S. The original demand curve is D_1. When the price of new cars rises, then demand for second-hand cars increases. The demand curve shifts from D_1 to D_2 and the price of second-hand cars increases from P_1 to P_2.

Whether the customer buys new or second-hand, from the moment of purchase the value of the car begins to depreciate (lose value). Cars have what is known as 'built-in obsolescence'. They will not last forever; they deteriorate by rusting and general wear and tear. You can try to make a car last as long as possible, but all the time its value depreciates, and manufacturers are constantly trying to persuade you to sell your existing car and buy another by heavy expenditure on persuasive advertising of new models. They regularly produce new models which cause existing models to appear 'dated'.

Each manufacturer of cars has a broad selection of models. With such a large selection the public can easily get confused, wondering which car to buy. There are five main groups of model:

SMALL CAR
SMALL FAMILY CAR
LARGE FAMILY CAR
ESTATE CAR
PRESTIGE CAR

(a) Small car

These are often run as a 'second' car by families. They are economical in their petrol consumption, and manoeverable around town. In the early 1970s there was a 500% increase in oil prices and since then more people have looked for fuel economy. Therefore these small cars are in high demand and in some cases worth more than larger models. When new these cars cost £3,500 to £5,000 and they keep their value well when they become second-hand.

(b) Small family cars

These cars are also economical to run, and are attractive to families as they are relatively small but easy to drive. When new their price ranges from £4,500 to nearly £7,000. Again they keep their value well.

(c) Large family cars

These cars generally have four doors (five in a hatchback version). They can accommodate easily a family of five. New prices range from £6,000 to £8,000 but due to higher running costs they lose their value more quickly than smaller cars and might therefore be cheaper than a smaller car of the same age. (If a car is known to have high running costs, this might deter the buyer and so the asking price might be lower). On the other hand, the engines of larger cars are easier to work on as there is more engine space and parts are more accessible, so they might be attractive to people who do their own servicing.

(d) Estate cars

These are extremely spacious cars, some with three rows of seats, capable of accommodating seven or eight people. New prices are high, ranging from £8,500 to £13,000. At the moment there is a relatively limited supply, which would tend to keep second-hand prices up, but demand is restricted to a rather narrow market, so they might be quite hard to sell.

(e) Prestige cars

These are either sports or luxury cars made for the rich. Prices start at about £15,000. The fuel consumption and running costs are high, but this probably doesn't worry the owner because these cars are not bought for economy in the first place. Some of these cars are collector's items, so unlike most second-hand cars which depreciate as they get older, many of these models appreciate, i.e. increase in value.

CHAPTER SIX KEVIN'S ASSIGNMENT: THE PRICE OF SECOND-HAND CARS

Five large car manufacturers have a car in the first four of the categories listed above. These are shown in Figure 6.5.

Manufacturer	Small car	Small family car	Large family car	Estate Car
Citröen	Dyane	AX	BX	CX
Austin Rover	Metro	Maestro	Montego	Rover 820
Ford	Fiesta	Escort	Sierra	Granada
Vauxhall	Nova	Astra	Cavalier	Carlton
Volkswagen	Polo	Golf	Jetta	Passat

Fig 6.5

2 Age

If second-hand cars were offered for sale at the same price as brand-new versions fo the same model, then demand for second-hand cars would be zero. It therefore stands to reason that second-hand cars are cheaper. Using economic theory, we can see from Figure 6.6 the demand curve for cars shifting to the left as cars become older. As a 'new' car becomes 'used' the demand curve shifts from D_1 to D_2 and the price falls from P_n to P_u. If we take for example a 1.3 litre, three-door Metro (Fig 6.7).

> **Good. Again using theory to explain the point you have made**

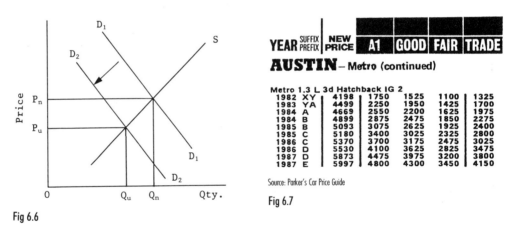

Fig 6.6

Fig 6.7

In Britain, buyers can tell the age of the car by looking at the registration letter. The graph in Figure 6.8 shows how this car depreciates as the car gets

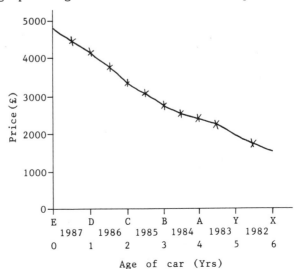

Fig 6.8

> **Excellent use of your graph**

older. The graph is very interesting, as people usually say that cars depreciate most in their first couple of years. We would therefore expect the graph to be steeper in the earlier years and then flatten out. However, this graph suggests that the price of the second-hand car is more or less proportional to the car's age. I think that the graphs in Figures 6.9a), b), c) and d) tend to support my hypothesis that smaller cars keep their value better than larger ones as they get older. As you move from a) through to d) (smaller cars to larger cars) you will notice the difference between new and second-hand prices increasing. Of course, it does not always follow that an old car is a poor car (or a new one is a good one). We must look at other factors also.

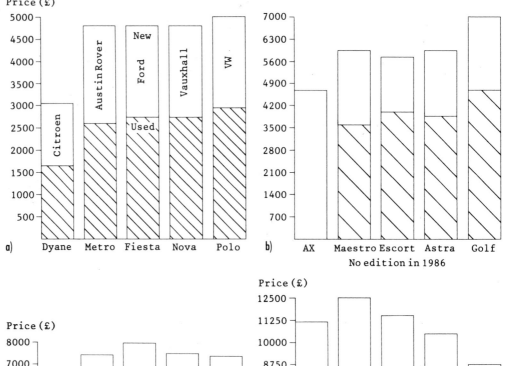

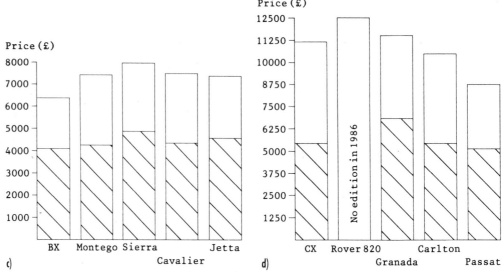

Fig 6.9

3 Mileage

Every car has a mileometer on the dashboard. 'Clocking' the mileometer (tampering with it to turn back the mileage) is illegal, and moder mileometers are tamper-proof. Private sellers often use vague phrases like 'average mileage'. People I have spoken to seem to regard about 9,000 miles per year as average. However, the type of mileage is also important because 9,000 miles of motorway driving with a gentle driver might be less punishing than the same mileage around town with an aggressive driver. Generally, a high mileage will lower the price of the car.

4 Condition

Advertisers usually include a phrase about the condition of the car, e.g. fair condition, good condition, very good condition, immaculate, or very clean car. Obviously, these phrases could mean almost anything, and it is up to potential

CHAPTER SIX KEVIN'S ASSIGNMENT: THE PRICE OF SECOND-HAND CARS

buyers to examine the bodywork, underside, interior and engine, and assess the condition for themselves. Clearly, the better the condition the higher the price.

5 Colour

> **This is rather vague. *Some* people might prefer yellow.**

This seems to be an important selling point; some garages make a point of describing the colour (Fig 6.10). People seem to prefer a blue or red car rather than pink or gold. Even people who say that they are not bothered about colour would probably be reluctant to drive a bright yellow car. A popular colour will help increase price.

> **Some attempt to try to explain *why* would assist in earning marks under 'analysis'.**

Fig 6.10

I interviewed the owner of Club Car Sales, and he was kind enough to answer my questions:

Q Why do you always mention the colour of your cars in your advertising?
A I don't know... it takes up a lot of space, and newspaper space is expensive... I suppose the colour of the car is an important factor in determining the price of the car. Some colours don't sell very well. For instance, base colour green is supposed to be unlucky.

Q Do you think colour is more important than mileage or condition?
A No, but with some cars the colour is a boost.

Q Do you think it helps having a filling station next to you?
A Yes, it won't make your sales soar. It's convenient... it's handy, put it that way. People see the cars when they come to buy petrol.

Q How many cars on average do you sell in a week.
A Well, on average about 10 or 11 a week.

The garages often inlcude the different shades of colour. But do you know the difference between Rosso, Armadine and Mexico Red? They are quite confusing. Private sellers normally state the colour, not the shade.

6 Extras

Extras are important to the motor car industry because the represent 'added value'. A car with a number of extras can sell at a higher price than a basic model. I suspect that the increase in price is greater than the actual cost of incorporating the extras. Sometimes the name of a model is a guide to the amount of added value that can be expected. For example:

```
     NISSAN          SUNNY           1.6            SLX
     maker           model           capacity       extras
```

```
NISSAN                        NEW SUNNY RANGE

Micra 1.0 L 3d                1.3 L 3d             1.6 SGX 4d
Micra 1.0 SG    3d            1.3 LX 3d            1.6 SGX 4d Auto
Micra 1.0 SG    3d Auto       1.3 LX 4d            1.6 SGX 5d
Micra 1.0 SG    5d            1.3 LX 5d            1.6 SGX 5d Auto
Micra 1.0 SG    5d Auto       1.6 LX 4d            1.7 LX Diesel 4d
Micra 1.0 Colette 3d          1.6 LX 5d            1.7 LX Diesel 5d
Micra 1.0 Colette 5d          1.6 SLX 4d           1.6 Coupe
                              1.6 SLX 4d Auto      1.6 ZX 16 valve Coupe
                              1.6 SLX 5d           1.6 LX Estate 5d
                              1.6 SLX 5d Auto
```

Fig 6.11

A Nissan car with an 'L' letter after its name is the basic model (Fig 6.11). The more letters after the name, the greater the number of extras. Here are just some of the extras that can be obtained, in different permutations:

Radio/stereo system   Tinted windows
Burglar alarm system   Spotlights
Sunroof   Spoilers
Electric windows   Anti-lock brakes
Central locking   Fuel injection
                               Automatic transmission

Hatchback versions are very popular at the moment, as the third or fifth door is very convenient for shopping and other family uses.

7 Terms of repayment

Large garages have realised that many people who buy cars need a loan. These garages have become Licensed Credit Brokers. The buyer should look carefully at the Annual Percentage Rate of Interest (APR). In economic terms, the availability of credit is a 'complement'. A fall in the price of a complement increases demand, therefore lower interest rates would shift the demand for cars to the right. The effect of a rightward-shift in demand is shown in Figure 6.4.

Some manufacturers and garages include interest rates as an important feature of their advertising (Fig 6.12). As you can see, the finance aspect is very prominently advertised. Private sellers and auctioneers cannot compete in this type of marketing. They offer a lower price, with no credit.

Fig 6.12

8 Prestige

Status symbol goods (or 'Veblen' goods as they are known, after an economist who studied them) do not conform to the same 'economic laws' as other goods. They are bought not only for their own sake, but for their effect on other people. They are items of 'conspicuous consumption'. I have read that the Porsche is actually not a very good car to drive. However, perhaps you don't buy a car like this for its driving qualities. I suppose that you buy it in order to park it outside your house and impress or annoy your neighbours!

> Yes, this kind of consumer psychology is very relevant to goods, like cars, which many people tend to regard as 'status symbols'.

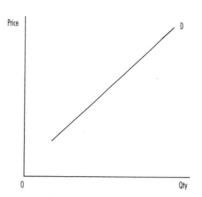

Fig 6.13

I have also heard it said that if you have to ask the price of a Rolls-Royce, then you probably can't afford one. It is possible that Rolls-Royces and Porsches have 'Perverse Demand Curves', sloping upwards from left to right (Fig 6.13). This shows that as the price of the good increases, the quantity of the demand also increases, thus breaking the usual law of demand. Unfortunately I do not know many owners of such cars, so I cannot say whether this demand curve is just a possibility, or whether it is a fact.

9 Cost of living in an area

> Lower levels of unemployment and higher levels of income are probably the main factors.

One area might have different car prices to another due to higher inflation in that area. This is so of South East England. Since housing prices have soared in this area and a car is the second purchase after a houise, car prices have also risen. This has lead to regions such as South Wales having cheaper cars than the South East, by some £100–£500. Wage differences also come into it, as a higher wage level will increase demand.

10 Warranty and MOT

Garages give a warranty (guarantee) if you purchase a car. Some private sellers have a period of time left on the new car warranty when they sell second-hand. However, usually neither private sellers nor auctions provide a warranty.

The MOT (Ministry of Transport) test is an important factor when advertising older models. The buyer will want the car to have passed its MOT as recently as possible, otherwise a lower price will be expected.

11 Speed and insurance group

The prestige cars are the fastest ones. Although their top speed is not stressed in advertisements (due to the national speed limit) it can be found in car performance magazines, and acceleration is mentioned.

However, sporty and faster cars belong to a higher insurance group number. Speed makes the chances of an accident more likely. Also, the prestige cars are more expensive to repair than the mass-produced family cars.

Insurance groups range from 1 to 9, higher groups being more expensive to insure. A Metro City 1.0 L model can attain a top speed of 86 mph, and belongs to Group 1, while a Porsche with a top speed of 170 mph belongs to Group 9. Clearly, buyers should consider the group before buying a car, as it has a significant effect on the 'on-the-road' price of a car. This means that buying the car is one thing, but before you can put it on the road you have to pay for further items such as tax and insurance. The road tax is the same for all cars, but the insurance is not. In effect, insurance increases the price of a car, and it is a cost which will be repeated each year.

12   The number of previous owners

It is much better to buy a car if you know its history. Advertisers, especially private sellers, usually mention how many previous owners the car had. Lady owners have a reputation of being more careful with their cars so 'one lady owner' is regarded as a selling point. People also like the previous owner to have been 'local'. If the number of owners is more than two, this is never mentioned as it is bound to depress the asking price, because people tend to assume that if a car has had one driver it will have suffered less damage than if it has been driven by many people.

13   Whether the car is British

Nowadays car companies are multi-national and it is difficult to define what is meant by a 'British' car. If you buy a Ford or a Vauxhall, for example, you might find that it was built in France, Spain, Germany, or elsewhere although important components may have been made in Britain. Some people believe that foreign cars have a better finish than British ones, and that many extras that appear to be 'optional' on British models are 'standard' on imported ones. Other people believe quite strongly that you should 'buy British'.

Probably the main thing to consider when looking at second-hand cars is the cost of spare parts, repairs and maintenance. These can be much higher for foreign cars, and so what the buyer saves on purchasing the car is gradually lost as the car is used on the road.

In the adverts which I have studied, British cars seem to be slightly dearer than foreign cars of a similar model.

Conclusions

In economic theory, the price of a new article is closely related to the costs of production. These costs are not so relevant when the article is re-sold, so putting a price on a second-hand article is always a difficult task. Very often the 'correct' price is simply the price that people are willing to pay or 'what the market will bear'. I think I have proved that there are certain factors which influence the price of a car, especially on the demand side.

On the supply side, I have shown which factors the three types of sellers consider important.

By conducting a survey I have drawn graphs to support my hypothesis that small cars lose their value more slowly than larger cars.

Problems encountered

When I was completing my graphs I was disappointed to find that some of the car models that I had found out a brand new price for where not available two years ago and so there is no second-hand price for these models.

The two interviews I conducted went well. The owners were very helpful, and very interested in my project. I gained my data from the South Wales Echo, the Western Mail, and Parker's Car Price Guide. Luckily, the project went smoothly.

GENERAL EXAMINER COMMENTS

We think that Kevin has done very well. He shows that he is fluent in the language of economics, and that he has used his studies to gain an insight into the way in which an aspect of the economy (the second-hand car market) works. Kevin demonstrates a good awareness of how economic concepts relate to the world around him. He rarely misses an opportunity to refer to a relevant piece of economic theory.

The project is well-informed and well written. If we have a criticism it is that he could perhaps have interviewed some buyers as well as sellers, possibly asking them to place the factors

CHAPTER SIX KATH'S ASSIGNMENT: LOCATION AND COMPETITION

influencing them in order of importance. Incidentally, 'car prices' is not an exclusively male topic; we have seen several good projects along these lines done by females.
The diagrams and press cuttings are relevant, and well integrated with the text. The initiative shown by Kevin in conducting interviews is also encouraging. If we were to use the mark-scheme for WJEC 'Fieldwork' on this project we would give the following marks:

Understanding and communication: 5 (out of 5).
Analysis and interpretation: 4 (out of 5).
Evaluation: 4 (out of 5).
Autonomy: 5 (out of 5).
TOTAL: 18 (out of 20) = 90%

Look at the 'Levels of Performance' on pages 56–7 and see if you agree.

UNIT 2 KATH'S ASSIGNMENT: LOCATION AND COMPETITION

Location and Competition

Introduction

I have taken three businesses: small, medium and large, and investigated their locations in the Bridgend area.

Aim

The question I wish to answer is: why are these businesses located on their respective sites and what competition do they have?

Method

I will try to find out why the owners or managers of these businesses believe that they have a good location. The three businesses I will write about are:

Ferrari's — cafe and bakery (small firm);
Wason's — decorating, wallpaper and DIY business (medium-sized firm);
Ford — motor vehicle manufacturer (large firm).

> *You should state what you mean by 'small', 'medium' and 'large' when describing firms such as these.*

Chapter 1: Ferrari's Bakery and Cafe

This is a bakery situated on the northern part of Bridgend town centre. It consists of two storeys with a bakery and shop on the ground floor and a cafe on the first floor. The bakery and cafe are in a good location as there are many customers and high sales. The advantages of this location are as follows:

(a) This location has a prime site as it is just across the road from the bus station. Those workers and shoppers who travel by bus must pass the bakery and cafe in order to reach the centre of Bridgend. Therefore the shop has many potential customers due to the bus station.

(b) The bakery is next to a pedestrian precinct which has many people walking past, sitting on the public benches, or using the precinct's telephone cabins.

(c) In a recent Geography class I took part in a count of the number of pedestrians passing at certain points in the town centre. I have decided to use the information we gathered for my Economics project also.
On that morning between 10 o'clock and 10.30, there were 221 pedestrians counted going through the 'York Passage' pedestrian precinct. This gives the bakery an average of 74 potential customers per minute — or more than 1 per second. Since this survey was carried out at fairly quiet times in the town the count may be much higher at other times. This proves that the cafe and bakery has a good position.

(d) There is a long tradition of Italian cafes in South Wales towns. Names like Cavalli, Sidoli, Servini and Ferrari have featured in the economy of South Wales since the industrial revolution. These cafes are generally family businesses whose members are well integrated into the local communities, and they are highly thought of by their customers. Consumer loyalty is likely to be very strong.

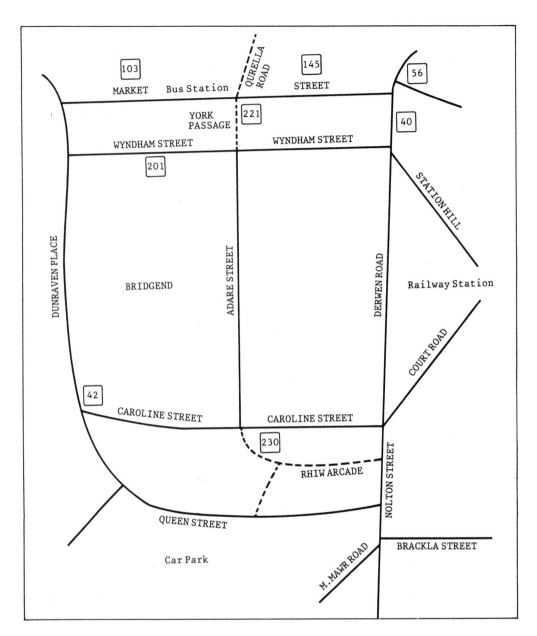

KEY
Figures in boxes signify the pedestrian flow figures counted in 30 minutes

Fig 6.14
Map showing the pedestrian flow figures at the competing shop locations

(e) Staff recruitment should not be a problem in Bridgend. Catering is taught in local schools and colleges, so there should be a pool of skilled labour for the bakery.
Apart from the full-time staff, there is also a large population of younger people, including students, willing to work part-time as waiters or waitresses.

(f) There are also advantages of having a bakery and a cafe on the same site. This means the bakery and cafe are integrated which carries many advantages:

  (i)   The bakery allows the cafe to have a flexible and cheap supply of bread and cakes.
  (ii) The bread and cakes can be baked according to the demand in the cafe and shop.
  (iii) The bread bought by the customer is fresh which is preferred to packaged bread.
  (iv) The integrated site cuts costs of transporting produce to the bakery every day. Flour and yeast and other raw materials must be delivered in bulk. The costs of production are cut considerably compared with the costs which would be incurred if the site was split.

There are some disadvantages to this location:

  (i)   There are bad parking facilities for customers with cars, and for delivery vans.

> **Figures 6.14 and 6.15 are nice maps but little direct use is made of them in the text. Try to use your data**

(ii) Market Street is a busy road which causes traffic noise within the bakery and cafe.
(iii) It is very close to competing bakeries and cafes like Astey's, the Cosy Cafe, and the Ogmore Vale Bakery, as shown on my map in Figure 6.15. However, the pedestrian flow survey shows that Ferrari's passing trade is similar to that of its competitors.

KEY
1 Ferrari's
2 Bus Station Cafe
3 Astey's
4 Cosy Cafe
5 Ogmore Vale Bakery
6 Conti's
7 Gregg's

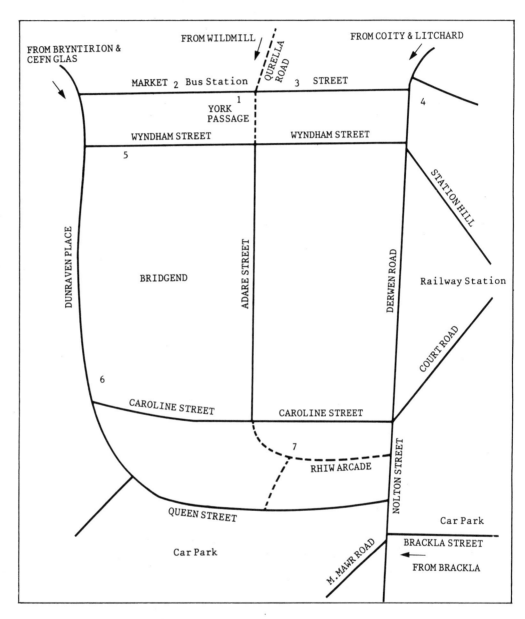

Fig 6.15
Map showing Ferrari's bakery and cafe and its competition and transport facilities

Chapter 2: Wason's DIY

This is number 1 on Figure 6.16 and is a medium-sized store specialising in wallpapers, paint, etc. Its location offers some advantages:

(i) There is a car park on Tremains Road just around the corner. However, this is a 'long-term' car park and charges are relatively high, so it is difficult to determine whether this is an advantage.
(ii) It is centrally placed between the bus station and railway station.
(iii) There is a large floorspace area to display DIY goods.

There are also some disadvantages:
(i) The pedestrian survey showed that the area was relatively quiet during the survey period. The shop depends on customers who deliberately set out to go there, rather than passing trade.
(ii) Vans and lorries delivering supplies have to park on a dangerous corner.
(iii) Customers coming by car will have to pay for parking at the municipal car park.

> **You don't seem to be sure whether the car parking facilities are good or bad.**

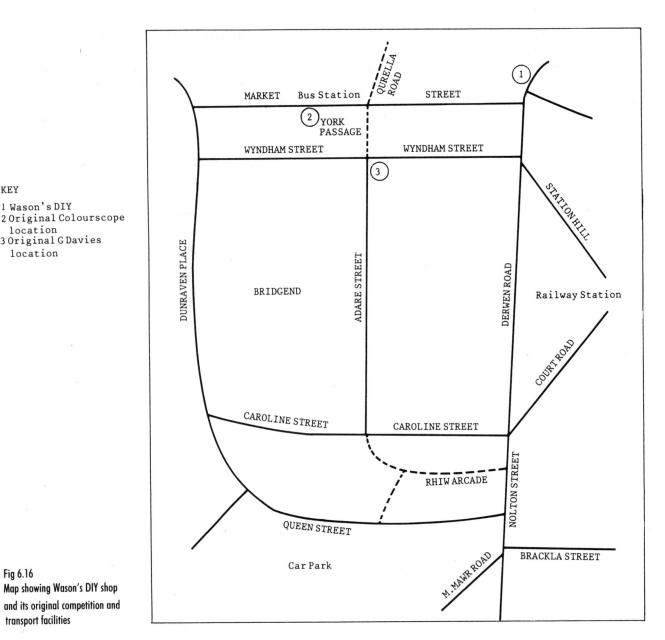

KEY
1 Wason's DIY
2 Original Colourscope location
3 Original G Davies location

Fig 6.16
Map showing Wason's DIY shop and its original competition and transport facilities

In spite of the disadvantages, within the town itself, competition to Wason's is practically non-existent. However, on the outskirts of Bridgend there is a large and thriving B&Q warehouse, on the Royal London Industrial Park. B&Q offers a much wider variety of goods at cheaper prices, together with free parking. The popularity of out-of-town shopping of this type must be causing problems for traders in the town centre.

Wason's has had competition within the town centre in the past from two shops: Colourscope and G. Davies Wallpapers (both in Wyndham Street), and there is some overlap of products with Bridgend Ironmongers in Derwen Road. Since G. Davies closed eight years ago, and Colourscope one year ago there is a near monopoly for DIY products within the town centre.

DIY is an expanding market, with more and more people owning their own houses and choosing to do their own decorating (see my interview with a representative of Wason's). I therefore think that the actual location of Wason's is not crucial; their business would not be significantly affected if they moved anywhere else within the town centre, as shoppers for most of what they sell have nowhere else to go unless they have a car and can go to B&Q.

Interviews

To help me study the location of Wason's I firstly interviewed Mr. Gwyn Davies. Together with his sister he owned the G. Davies wallpaper and paint shop at the junction of Wyndham Street and Adare Street. It closed in 1980 on their retirement.

CHAPTER SIX KATH'S ASSIGNMENT: LOCATION AND COMPETITION

Q Did you compete fiercely with Wason's shop?
A Yes, for let's see, nearly twenty years.

Q Do you think that Wason's has a favourable location?
A No, in many ways our location was better. Wason's is on a busy main road without many pedestrians passing. The building was originally the cooperative store, and when they acquired a new site Wason's was able to acquire the old shop at a favourable price.

Q Is the decoration business a very competitive selling area?
A Yes, it always has been. There have been bankruptcies in businesses of this type in this area.

Q Do you like the idea of a monopoly now that Colourscope has closed?
A No, a monopoly isn't a good thing for the seller or for the buyer. One shop usually isn't capable of handling all the business. Without competition there might be less innovation, falling standards and higher prices.

Q Did you regularly monitor the prices at Wason's?
A Yes, we kept an eye on them. We also watched their selling methods, and in the 1970s, for example, we both went over to self-service at about the same time. This was what the customers wanted, and it reduced our labour costs.

I then interviewed a representative of Wason's about their location in Bridgend:

Q Do you consider your shop to have a favourable location in Bridgend?
A Yes, I think it is fairly good, but could be better.

Q How many employees have you?
A At this branch we have five full time staff.

Q Since Gwyn Davies and Colourscope have closed down Wason's has become the only wallpaper and paints shop in the centre of Bridgend. Do you think it is good to have a local monopoly in the town centre?
A The customer should have a choice, but this can be done within a shop.

Q Who do you view as your competitor now?
A I think B&Q is definitely our main competitor. Tesco used to deal in paint and were quite competitive, but they have stopped.

Q Would you like a location closer to the centre of town if the opportunity arose in the future?
A Yes, most definitely, especially closer to the main car parks. However, such sites are hard to find nowadays.

Q Do you consider your parking facilities to be adequate?
A No. We could do with the car park around the corner becoming a free car park. At the moment parking is too expensive. When the car park attendants went on strike and the car parking was free, the sales in every shop in Bridgend doubled in that period.

Q Have your sales increased since G. Davies and Colourscope closed?
A Yes, definitely.

Chapter 3: Ford Engine Plant

This is a large car plant situated at the Waterton Industrial Estate just outside Bridgend. This was a greenfield site selected by Ford from several sites in Britain and Europe in order to make engines for its cars. There are several advantages which must have influenced Ford management to choose Bridgend:

(a) There are very good transport links, with the closeness of the M4 motorway a deciding factor. British Rail also built a spur linking the plant with the main South Wales railway line, so that components could be moved in and engines moved out by train. Ford regarded this railway link with its other factories as a 'long-distance conveyor belt'.
(b) The land is a large flat area with room for future expansion.

(c) There are good housing facilities nearby for Ford workers.
(d) The engine plant is in an area with a skilled workforce.
(e) Ford is a 'footloose' firm and is not tied to a particular location by raw material or power source.
(f) Bridgend had Special Development Area status at the time of the decision to locate. This qualified the plant to receive grants and tax allowances. The Prime Minister at the time, James Callaghan, was Member of Parliament for a nearby constituency in Cardiff. He took a personal interest in the Ford decision and encouraged Ford management to choose the Bridgend site with the provision of extra 'discretionary' grants on top of the ones they were entitled to.

Economies of Scale at Bridgend

(i) Other factories within the Ford Group are accessible via the M4 and by rail.
(ii) The plant currently employs 1491 people. There is considerable scope for specialisation and automation, with the use of robots.
(iii) The site is large with 189 acres of flat land. There is 2.5 miles of roadway on site, with 1.75 miles of railway.
(iv) Cardiff and Swansea docks are equi-distant from the plant. Engines for the Escort and Orion can easily be shipped.
(v) The area is within easy reach of both Swansea and Cardiff University Colleges, the Polytechnic of Wales, and Bridgend College of Technology, giving ample opportunities for the education and training of workers.
(vi) Due to the government grants the set-up costs were £101.5 million instead of £145 million.

> **You could have explained a bit more clearly why each of these are economies of scale, and classified them as either 'internal' or 'external'. You also need to say what is meant by 'multiplier effects'.**

Multiplier Effects

(a) All but approximately 50 of the 1491 employees were hired locally. This clearly increased incomes in the Bridgend area.
(b) There have been estimates that a further 2000 jobs have been created as a direct result of the Ford expansion, through increased trade for local shops, more housing etc. However, these estimates have been made by journalists, and have not yet been verified by economists.
(c) The Ford Plant is on the border of two county council areas: Mid Glamorgan and South Glamorgan, and also on the border of two district council areas: Ogwr and The Vale of Glamorgan. Local authority income from the Business Rate is therefore widely spread.

Competition

The Ford Plant does not face the same type of competition as the other two businesses I have studied, since this a manufacturing industry while the others are retail. The considerations affecting the siting of the Ford Plant are not quite the same as those affecting the siting of a shop.
However, the end result of Ford operations is the selling of motor cars. About a mile from the Ford plant is the premises of the main Ford dealer in Bridgend, and this is the shop window for Ford products.

> **There is fierce competition in the market for cars both at home and overseas.**

If Ford chooses its most efficient locations for all its manufacturing operations, then eventually the price of Ford models in the showrooms will be reduced. It is important for the car industry to be competitive. As the single European market approaches in 1992, competition between car manufacturers will be even more intense, and it will be even more important that manufacture should take place at efficient locations.

Conclusion

Different types of business have different types of influences to consider when choosing a location.
Ferrari's and Ford appear to have locations which suit their particular needs. The location of Wason's could be better, but once established at a site, and operating successfully, it becomes difficult to move. This is what economics textbooks refer to as industrial intertia.

> **This highlights the importance of starting your coursework early.**

```
Acknowledgements
I would like to thank the people who agreed to be interviewed. Unfortunately, in
spite of several attempts, I was unable to arrange an interview with a
representative of Ferrari's. I simply couldn't find a time when business was
slack enough to be able to talk to the owner.
Information on Ford was obtained from 'Ford Facts', a publication provided by
the company.
```

GENERAL EXAMINER COMMENTS

Kath obtained an overall Grade 'A' in GCSE Economics, but we think this must have been mainly due to an outstanding performance on her written papers, as we do not regard this piece of coursework as Grade A material. It represents a middle level of achievement: somewhere around grade 'C'.

It is interesting and well-written, and her interviews contain some very sensible and relevant questions, but we think there are several ways in which this work could have been improved. It seems to us that there should have been more *negotiation* between Kath and her teacher during the early stages, in order to pick a more logical selection of businesses. We can see a logic in going for a small, medium and large business, but we cannot see the point of studying two shops and a manufacturer. It does not compare like with like.

We cannot stress too strongly the importance of *seeking advice*. Do not be afraid that by asking your teacher questions you will make yourself look stupid, or lacking in initiative. Teachers often find that it is the students without initiative who go their own sweet way, while it is the students with initiative who seek guidance, because they ask questions which show that they are thinking for themselves. For example, if Kath had asked 'Which three firms should I study?' she would have been asking the teacher to do her thinking for her. But if she asked 'Do you think these three are suitable examples of small, medium and large firms?' then the teacher can help while being able to see that Kath is thinking for herself. This gives the teacher an opportunity to perhaps show Kath some ways in which she could improve her choice.

The siting of Ford at Bridgend is a large topic which is worth a piece of coursework in itself. In the context of this project, we think Kath would have been better advised to look at a large shop to contrast either with Ferrari's or Wason's. For instance, she could have studied the out-of-town location of the B&Q store which she mentions at several points in her work, and this should have yielded some interesting comparisons with the two town-centre sites. The overall impression is one of three different case studies, without much of a common theme.

Having said all that, however, there is quite a bit of economics in Kath's project, although the different strands could perhaps have been better drawn together, and there are some missed opportunities. For instance, perhaps she could have followed up the remarkable claim that turnover doubled when car parking was free – there would have been quite a bit of economic mileage in a study of this through questioning shoppers at town centre and out-of-town locations. Cafe owners are very busy people and the fact that Kath could not arrange an interview at a mutually suitable time illustrates one of the difficulties of coursework. We also wonder whether or not she tried to obtain an interview with a Ford representative.

Nevertheless, don't forget that GCSE examiners are under strict instructions to mark *positively*, and Kath has shown what she knows, understands, and can do, so we think she would receive a respectable mark, but not as high as Kevin's in the previous assignment. By the way, did you notice how Kath made use of information which she had previously collected as part of a Geography project? We think that was a very sensible thing to do, since the information was very relevant. Looking for 'cross curricular themes' is a very desirable educational exercise, and it helps you to avoid becoming overloaded with coursework if you can use some of the information you collect more than once in subjects which are related. Using the SEG mark scheme we would award Kath something along these lines:

Information: 3 (out of 4).
Analysis: 4 (out of 8).
Evaluation: 3 (out of 8).
Presentation: 3 (out of 5).

TOTAL: 13 (out of 25) = 52%.

UNIT 3 KIM'S ASSIGNMENT: ADVERTISING

Advertising

Aim
I have tried to answer the question: 'How and why do the advertising activities of large firms differ from the advertising activities of small firms?'

Methods
In an attempt to prove that the advertising activities of large firms and small firms are different, I have used textbooks, my own knowledge, a questionnaire (Fig 6.17a), a survey of TV adverts, and a survey of local, regional and national newspapers. I did the TV survey over a one-day period, but it was mainly in the evening as I was at school during the day.

> 66 The survey might not be very representative, being only one day. 99

Findings
Advertising is an amazingly expensive thing to do. So small firms are rather limited. Advertising campaigns differ because the fierce competition of firms to sell their product forces each firm to work to the best of its ability to beat their competition. Large firms can usually afford to advertise on television.

> 66 Very vague – give some specific details. In any case, some advertising is relatively cheap. 99

Out of the ten people to whom I put my questionnaire, five people mentioned television advertising as the form they most frequently noticed (see Fig 6.17). One said that TV and magazine adverts were equally noticeable. Another five said that they often leave the room during commercial breaks. Thus it seems that large and small firms are at an equal advantage.

> 66 But 50% of the people stay in the room during the commercials, and these are reached by large firms, as small firms don't advertise on television. 99

Questioned whether they would buy a plastic bag when out shopping three out of ten said yes. Therefore these people are willing to pay a large firm money in order to advertise their product. It is most unlikely that they would buy a small paper bag from a small firm.

Posters and billboards are expensive for small firms, although perhaps they can sometimes afford to put up posters for a small length of time.

Radio advertising is a possibility for small firms, but only local radio. National radio does not have advertising.

> 66 Very vague. Presumably shoppers buy large quantities of goods from large retailers and therefore require carrier bags (which are given freely by some shops). 99

1. Which form of advertising do you most frequently notice?
   (a) Television
   (b) Radio
   (c) Billboards
   (d) Papers
   (e) Plastic bags
   (f) Other

> 66 Surely radio advertising is more expensive than billboards? 99

2. When an advert comes on the T.V., do you
   (a) Watch
   (b) Leave the room

3. Has advertising ever made you aware of a new product?
   (a) Yes
   (b) No

4. When shopping would you but a plastic bag?
   (a) Yes
   (b) No

5. Can you name a small firm which advertises on T.V.?
   (a) Yes
   (b) No

Fig 6.17 (a) Questionnaire

Out of a sample of 10 friends and neighbours, the results of the Questionnaire were

1 (a) 5
   (b) 3
   (c) 0
   (d) 2
   (e) 0
   (f) 0
2 (a) 5
   (b) 5
3 (a) 9
   (b) 1
4 (a) 3
   (b) 7
5 (a) 0
   (b) 10

Fig 6.17 (b)

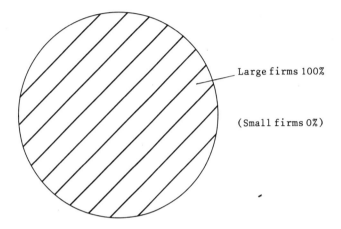

Pie Chart to show the percentage of TV adverts placed by large and small firms over a one-day period.

Fig 6.17 (c)

> **You need to collect specific information about costs, and attempt to analyse the *effectiveness* of advertising. Assertions are being made here without any evidence to back them up.**

In the national papers large adverts would be very expensive and so their adverts are from large firms. Local papers have more advantages for small firms.

To conclude this study I would say that small firms advertise locally while large firms advertise nationally (Fig 6.17c). This is because small firms:

(a) cannot afford expensive advertising costs;
(b) some small firms would be too busy if they advertised and could not cope with more customers.

GENERAL EXAMINER COMMENTS

This project has a number of serious faults. It is poorly organised; Kim does not seem to have been working to a synopsis or 'battle plan'. Terms are introduced without being defined (this was also a fault with Kath, to some extent: e.g. what exactly do economists mean by 'large' and 'small' when describing firms?)

The introduction mentions a newspaper survey, but no details appear in the text. Kim also mentions 'textbooks', but there is no evidence that textbooks have been used.

This topic is essentially concerned with economies of scale; a sensible approach would have been to examine what it is that economics textbooks have to say about advertising, and to look at the advantages of large firms over small firms in this sphere, then to test whether economic theory helps explain how firms actually behave.

Before embarking on a questionnaire, it is important to have clear aims in mind, and to have an idea of what you hope to achieve by asking questions. It is also important to consider *to whom* the questionnaire is addressed. It was always unlikely that the people Kim interviewed would have the knowledge required to be helpful to the assignment. For this particular topic a survey of a couple of people actually involved in running small and large businesses would be more helpful than a survey of any number of friends and neighbours. Kim's teacher would have been able to suggest suitable people to be approached.

The presentation of results is rather uninteresting. The last pie chart seems to be a waste of time. The purpose of a pie chart is to clearly convey information which perhaps cannot be so easily conveyed in any other way. If 100% of adverts are from large firms, then why not just say so? Drawing a pie chart is just an exercise done for its own sake, in this case.

It is very difficult for us to mark this project in a *positive* manner, because only Kim's class teacher is in a position to judge whether the poor outcome was an honest attempt by the student to work to the best of her ability, or whether it was the result of cutting corners and sheer laziness. It certainly underlines the importance of seeking advice, especially in the early stages. More teacher guidance might have pointed Kim along more rewarding paths.

Let us assume that from Kim's point of view this project represents a great deal of hard work, but that unfortunately, due to poor technique, it does not demonstrate or do justice to what Kim knows, understands and can do. We can therefore award *some* marks. We stress that we are giving low marks **not** because the assignment is a short one, but because its standard is low. If it had quality, then the lack of quantity would be less important. However, we think that to demonstrate quality and achieve all the assessment objectives will usually require a larger quantity of material than is given in this case.

Using the LEAG mark scheme we would give the following marks:

Treatment: 1 (out of 7).
Range of material: 2 (out of 5).
Analysis of material: 2 (out of 7).
Presentation: 3 (out of 7).
Economic ideas: 1 (out of 7).
TOTAL: 9 (out of 33) = 28%.

Kim now has a mountain to climb, in order to do well enough on the written papers to cancel out this bad performance. If you put some effort into your coursework it is time well spent: you will earn a 'platform' of marks which no-one can take away from you. We hope that you can avoid Kim's mistakes, so that when you sit your written papers you can build upon a solid foundation.

UNIT 4 KEN'S ASSIGNMENT: INTERNATIONAL TRADE

AIMS

I have two aims.

(1) To answer the question:
    How does international trade affect our everyday lives?

(2) To test the hypothesis:
    Even if we were able to produce all our own requirements, we would still import from overseas.

METHOD

In order to achieve these aims I set myself the following tasks.

(1) (a) I surveyed 19 items of clothing found in the wardrobes of my home, and discovered their countries of origin.

   (b) I drew up a typical daily menu (breakfast, lunch and evening meal) and showed which countries the food comes from.

CHAPTER SIX KEN'S ASSIGNMENT: INTERNATIONAL TRADE

(2) I used a questionnaire to find out why people buy imported goods, especially when we can produce them ourselves.

(3) I noticed that the 'Single European Market, 1992' was receiving a great deal of press and TV publicity. I therefore studied the EEC and the impact it has on UK trade.

(4) I chose a local firm and investigated ways in which it is involved in international trade.

RESULTS

Task 1: A Survey of Imported Goods in the Home

(a) Clothes

ITEM OF CLOTHING	COUNTRY (made by)
100% cotton trousers	Portugal
70% wool, 30% mixed fibres jacket	England
88% acrylic, 12% nylon jumper	Hong Kong
100% cotton sweater	India
100% cotton jeans	Hong Kong
100% cotton underwear	Great Britain
100% acrylic jumper	Korea
100% cotton skirt	Great Britain
100% acrylic jumper	Taiwan
100% leather jacket	England
mixed fibres trousers	Great Britain
100% cotton underwear	Israel
78% polyester, 22% cotton jacket	England
100% cotton underwear	Great Britain
50% cotton, 80% polyester top and skirt	Portugal
Mixed fibres jacket	England
80% acrylic, 20% nylon jumper	Korea
70% polyester, 30% viscose skirt	Great Britain
95% cotton, 5% elastane lycra underwear	Austria

Fig 6.18

```
E  = 4      K  = 2
GB = 5      Is = 1
P  = 2      T  = 1
HK = 2      A  = 1
In = 1
```

❝ It does not show this; there is confusion here over the terms 'England' and 'Britain'. A pie-chart would have been useful. ❞

The chart clearly shows that over 50% of the clothes were made abroad.

Although the sample is only a small cross-section, it does prove to a certain extent that many of the clothes we buy are not made in Great Britain. We are aiding other countries more than our own. We should buy British wherever possible to aid the economy and British manufacturers should try to produce a wider range of choice in the clothing they make. This might boost the sales of British products in the clothing industry.

❝ This is a bit vague. Look at what we say later about the 'Law of Comparative Advantage'. ❞

(b) Food

Despite the productivy of British farms, much foodstuff still has to be imported.

BREAKFAST	WHERE PURCHASED	COUNTRY
Toast (Bread)		Britain
Butter		New Zealand
Marmalade	Supermarket	Britain
Tea	e.g. Tescos	India
Milk		Britain
Sugar		Britain
Cornflakes		Britain

LUNCH	WHERE PURCHASED	COUNTRY
Chicken		Britain
Tomatoes		"
Coleslaw		"
Lettuce		"
Cucumber	Supermarket	"
Radish	e.g. Tescos	"
Carrot		"
Cottage Cheese		"
Orange Juice		"
Apple		South Africa
Biscuit		Britain

DINNER	WHERE PURCHASED	COUNTRY
Lamb Chops		New Zealand
Potatoes		Britain
Peas		Britain
Broccoli	Supermarket	"
Wine/Water	e.g. Tescos	Germany
Apple Pie		Britain
Cream		Britain

Fig 6.19
A Typical Daily Menu showing which foods come from which countries.

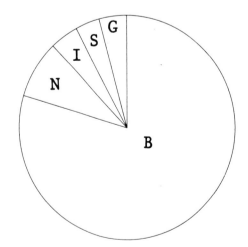

B Britain = $^{20}/_{25} \times 360° = 288°$
N New Zealand = $^{2}/_{25} \times 360° = 28.8°$
I India = $^{1}/_{25} \times 360° = 14.4°$
S S. Africa = $^{1}/_{25} \times 360° = 14.4°$
G Germany = $^{1}/_{25} \times 360° = 14.4°$

Fig 6.20
Results showing the comparison between British and Imported foods

Over three quarters of the food in the typical daily menu which I constructed comes from Britain. This is a significant difference from the proportion of clothing.

Task 2: Questionnaire

I designed a questionnaire and conducted a survey to try to find reasons why people bought imported goods, and whether they give any thought to the country of origin of the products they purchase.

QUESTIONNAIRE

This questionnaire aims to discover why people buy imported goods when we can produce them ourselves.

1) Do you buy imported goods?   YES _____   NO _____

2) Do you find that they are cheaper?   YES _____   NO _____

3) If you liked an item, would its origin affect your decision to buy?   YES _____   NO _____

4) Would you say imported goods are of better quality than British manufactured goods?   YES _____   NO _____

5) Would you say the technology of the majority of imported goods is more advanced?   YES _____   NO _____

6) If there were two identical objects, one was imported and the other from Britain, which would you buy? _____

7) Why would you make this choice? _____

8) Do you always buy a typical brand of electrical goods?   YES _____   NO _____

   If 'YES' name the brand. _____

9) Why do you think people buy imported goods? _____

From the questionnaire I devised which surveyed 9 people I found that:

Question
No.
- (1) 100% buy imported goods:
- (2) 66.6% find imported goods cheaper than British manufactured goods;
- (3) 88.8% said that the items origin would affect their decision to buy;
- (4) 11.1% said they thought that imported goods are of better quality than British manufactured goods, 11.1% said no; and 77.7% said it would depend on the item;
- (5) 77.7% said the technology of the majority of imported goods is more advanced:
- (6) 55.5% said they would choose British rather than foreign where an identical object was concerned.
  44.4% said they would choose the best value for money.

(7) 55.5% said they would make this choice to help British Economy;
(8) 66.6% always bought the same brand of electrical goods;
22.2% always bought Hotpoint – BRITISH
11.1% always bought Hoover – BRITISH
(9) 11.1% think people buy imported goods because of advertisements pushing them to do so,
33.3% thinks it is because they are of better quality and value for money,
44.4% say it is because they are cheaper, and
22.2% say it is because of the new ideas and different styles.

According to this questionnaire, everyone buys imported goods. This is because many people find that they are cheaper than our own British manufactured goods, and also they are often of better quality with new ideas and different styles.

Surprisingly, almost 90% said that the origin of an item would affect their decision to buy, South Africa was pointed out particularly. This is clearly related to the politics of that country. Where consumers deliberately avoid the products of a country due to political reasons this is known as a "consumer boycott". This shows that a large number of people do actually think about buying imported goods and don't just take them for granted.

> **This contradicts your earlier statement about quality.**

Only a small minority said that they thought imported goods are of better quality than British manufactured goods, the same percentage said "no" but the majority said that it would depend entirely on the item.

Over 50% indicated that if given a choice of two identical goods at the same price from different origins they would choose the British good, and this was to help the British economy.

My view is that people buy imported goods because they are, generally, cheaper, have a wider choice of designs and styles, and are well advertised. Clothes from places like Korea are cheaper because of lower labour costs in those countries. Certain foodstuffs, such as wine, can be produced in Britain, but are imported because of climatic conditions and other factors (Germany, for example, has a well established wine-making industry). The Law of Comparative Advantage is an economic theory which tells us that countries will specialise in goods and services at which they are most efficient, and will import other goods, even if they could in principle be domestically produced. Thus Britain could, in theory, be self-sufficient in bananas, but the costs would be high so we import from the West Indies.

> **The Law of Comparative Advantage is relevant here (see 'General' comments below).**

Task 3: Britain's Trade With the EEC

The aims and membership of the EEC

The aims of the EEC are to raise the living standards of the people of its member countries; to promote the freedom of movement of labour, capital and services; to reduce tariffs and trade restrictions between members, maintaining a common tarrif policy to non-members; and to encourage close cooperation between members in matters of commerce, farming, finance, social services, industry and legal systems. A long term political aim is to create a "United States of Europe".

The EEC was set up by the Treaty of Rome on 25 March 1957. Then, its members were France, West Germany, Italy, Belgium, The Netherlands, and Luxembourg. It was inspired by the success of an earlier organisation, the European Coal and Steel Community, which began in 1952. Britain, Eire and Denmark all joined in 1973. Spain, Portugal and Greece have also now joined, bringing the total membership up to twelve.

In response to the creation of the EEC, Austria, Iceland, Norway, Portugal, Switzerland, Sweden and Britain formed a rival group, the European Free Trade Area. EFTA was a much looser organisation, and in the end less successful (for example, they did not all match the increased living standards of the EEC, which by the 1970s had managed to raise the average purchasing power of its members' peoples by 75%). During the 1960s both Labour and Conservative governments tried to take Britain into the EEC, but it was Edward Heath, a Conservative Prime

CHAPTER SIX KEN'S ASSIGNMENT: INTERNATIONAL TRADE

Minister, who finally took Britain into the EEC on 1 January, 1973, after leaving EFTA.

The advantages and disadvantages of the EEC

There are many advantages of belonging to the EEC. It is much easier to travel to EEC countries — there are far less strict regulations on movement between countries, i.e. no visas are required to travel, customs regulations are unified. Postal services are coordinated, so a first-class British stamp is sufficient to have a letter delivered anywhere in the EEC by airmail. It is easier to work in EEC countries (Spain and Portugal being partly excepted since they have only just joined).

> **What about Greece?**

Farmers are allowed to produce as much as they can within quota limits and have it guaranteed to be brought up to a set price by the EEC if it cannot be sold. This enables farmers to be guaranteed an income, and so keeps them in business despite of fluctuations in demand and supply. The aim is to prevent shortages, so that if imported supplies of food dried up there would still be a home produced supply.

> **Does this benefit *all* countries, or just the member countries?**

The economic policy of free trade between members allows members to specialise in the industries where they have the greatest efficiency compared with other countries, thus producing goods at the cheapest prices, which follows the Law of Comparative Advantage and is to the benefit of all countries.

The members have a common tariff policy to non-members, thus in reply to proposed American tariffs in late 1987, the EEC threatened retaliation with counter-tariffs, and the USA dropped its proposals. Also, the EEC has been able to negotiate with the Japanese and persuade them to lower some of their traditionally high trade barriers. The EEC as an organisation has more economic "clout" and can negotiate from a stronger position than any of the individual countries could.

There is quite a complicated European legal system in existence. Unlike other international organisations, the EEC can enforce its laws directly on the citizens of member countries, without acting through the government of the individual country. It is therefore essential that people have direct access to European courts. Governments, companies, local authorities and private individuals can take cases to the relevant court when appropriate. This has disadvantages: for example, it adds a European layer of bureaucracy and red tape to economic and business affairs; but it also has advantages: for instance, people who find that their local beach is polluted might be able to use European law to make the polluter pay for cleaning, if they find that their domestic laws are too weak.

In order to make the operation of European laws and regulations more democratic, the EEC has a directly-elected parliament of "Euro" MPs. Unlike other parliaments, the European Assembly cannot pass laws, but rather it acts as a "watchdog". Euro MPs tend to concern themselves with issues such as consumer protection, environmental pollution, regional policy, and the activities of multinational monopolistic companies.

> **The source of these figures ought to be stated, and their accuracy checked.**

These are all economic issues which are likely to cause more and more political and social concern in the 1990s and so I would classify the existence of a Euro parliament as a definite advantage of membership of the EEC.

There are, conversely, disadvantages to membership. Of all the EEC countries, only France, West Germany and Britain actually pay more money to the EEC than they receive, and although West Germany is far wealthier than Britain, they both pay about the same, currently about £250 million per year.

> **But you said earlier that quotas were an *advantage* as they kept farmers in business!**

Also, farmers are limited to certain quotas of production, which is causing tremendous problems in, for instance, dairy farming, where families are having to leave businesses which they have built up over the generations.

> **Is this an advantage or disadvantage? You could argue that bringing things up to a European standard (e.g. cleaner car exhaust emissions) is beneficial.**

Countries have to adapt their own standards for various things to EEC standards, which may cause confusion, e.g. British sausages and chocolate do not come up to EEC standards. However, in the long term this will decrease confusion when trading or travelling between countries.

One benefit of the high fees Britain pays is that they are often redistributed to people who need them. For example, the EEC often funds projects to redevelop inner cities or run-down industrial areas, easing unemployment.

The effects of "1992"

The advertisements appearing in the press and on TV state that Europe is "open for business" in 1992. This means that by that time "harmonisation" will have taken a great leap forward amongl member countries. Customs barriers will be completely removed (apart from security checks for terrorists and health checks for such things as rabies), and there will be completely free movement, not only of goods, but also capital and labour. There is also pressure from the EEC commissioners to "harmonise" such things as professional qualifications, so that a doctor or a teacher, for example, could find work in any EEC country, and there is also pressure to harmonise tax rates — so that all member countries would, for instance, set common rates of VAT on such things as bottles of wine. At the moment there is resistance to some of these measures from national politicians, but as 1992 approaches this resistance might crumble as the moment of harmonisation gathers. At about the same time, the Channel Tunnel will be opened and changes in our educational system should ensure that all British schoolchildren learn a European language.

Years ago politicians such as Winston Churchill (Conservative) and Ernest Bevin (Labour) said taht they wanted to be able to travel across Europe without using a passport. Their dream might now be coming true, and leading to a type of "United States of Europe", the exact form of which we can only guess at today.

The Effect of International Trade on a Local Firm

Electro Acoustic Industries (ELAC) Ltd.

> **Some parts of this section do not appear to be written in your own words.**

ELAC is situated on the Bridgend Industrial Estate. This company is the major British specialist manufacturer of original equipment loudspeaker drive units supplying the international automotive, high fidelity, telecommunications, public address and general electronics industries. It was founded in 1946.

There are more than 400 employees at factories in London and South Wales. ELAC produces in excess of three million drive units annually and provides its customers with a service in the design and development of customised products meeting many different performance requirements and applications.

ELAC products are built to the highest levels of quality, each loudspeaker being individually tested for acoustic and mechanical precision before being being released from the factory and sophisticated quality control techniques are used to monitor each stage of assembly.

Parts which are used to make the speakers are purchased from various EEC countries and the Far East, including Taiwan and Japan. The reasons for buying from foreign countries include cost and availability. The firm tries to use parts from UK sources wherever possible. This is because the service is reliable and the reaction to problems and deliveries are much faster. Parts from the Far East can take too long to arrive, they can be at sea for up to eight weeks. It is too costly to transport the parts by air.

ELAC has customer in many nations. 30% of ELAC automotive speakers go abroad. Here is a list of destinations of finished products.

FORD
Halewood, Southampton (UK). Ghent (Belgium). Cologne (West Germany). Saarlouis (France). Valencia (Spain).

GENERAL MOTORS
Liverpool, Luton (UK). Russellheim (West Germany).

ROVER & HONDA
Cowley, Longbridge (UK). Tokyo (Japan).

ELAC also makes hi-fi speakers. They have the brand name TDL, which stands for Transducer Developments Ltd. This part of the firm has an office in New York to handle sales in the USA. Only 10% of TDL hi-fi speakers are sold in the UK, with

90% going overseas. TDL ship their hi-fi speakers to the following countries.

> UK
> GREECE
> BELGIUM
> WEST GERMANY
> ITALY
> SPAIN
> NORWAY
> AUSTRALIA
> THAILAND
> CANADA
> USA
> CANARY ISLES
> AUSTRIA
> SOUTH AFRICA
> TAIWAN
> ISTANBUL
> JAPAN
> NETHERLANDS
> CYPRUS
> EGYPT

> **Spot the odd ones in this list! 'Istanbul' is a city (the country is Turkey), and the 'Canary Isles' are strictly part of Spain. Be careful when mentioning exotic places.**

If the Pound Sterling is weak, people overseas will want to buy more UK goods. If Sterling is strong, people will want to buy fewer UK goods. This is because an increase in the value of the Pound against, say, the Dollar means that an American must use more Dollars in order to pay for a British good. Some economists believe that we should not use the words "weak" and "strong" to describe the Pound's exchange rate, because from the point of view of UK exporting industries a so-called "weak" Pound can be beneficial, and a "strong" Pound can be damaging.

The list shows that the managers of ELAC are interested in the foreign exchange rates of many countries, ranging from the Peseta to the Yen. There are also some considerable distances to be travelled, many languages to do business in and many different cultures, business methods, trading standards and laws from country to country. These are problems which do not arise in domestic trade. The company must feel that the advantages of large scale production and wider markets more than outweigh any disadvantages of trading overseas.

Conclusions

Britain was once known as the "workshop of the world" because it obtained raw materials, many of which were imported, and turned them into manufactured products which it then exported all over the globe. Britain was the world's main producer of manufactured goods. In recent times Britain has become more of a "service centre" than a "workshop". Our "visible" trade balance has suffered because although demand in Britain for manufactured goods is high, British industry has been unable to satisfy that demand and so these items are imported, giving us a "trade gap". In recent years there has been a "boom" in the shops, with industrial sites becoming "retail parks" and banks providing easily obtainable credit facilities which are expensive to the customer but profitable to the banks, due to the very high interest rates experienced in Britain in the late 1980s. In the absence of government controls, personal debt and consumer spending have spiralled. But the items being purchased in this so-called "boom" (cars, TV sets, record players, etc.) are overwhelmingly imported goods. People keep saying that Britain's future lies in the service sector, but while it is true that there is a demand for services, it is equally true that there is a strong demand for consumer goods. To me it seems a pity that we are sacrificing our role as a manufacturing nation to become a "nation of shopkeepers" selling imported goods.

Britain's surplus on the exporting and importing of "invisibles" (such things as banking services, insurance and tourism) have in the past been relied upon to make up for any visible deficit. In the 1970s Britain became a net exporter of oil and this to some extent disguised our poor performance in exporting manufactures. The strong pound resulting from our oil exports also had the effect of increasing the overseas prices of our exports, and making the job of our exporting industries that much harder.

Although free trade between nations might eventually bring prosperity due to national specialisation, there are many hurdles in the way. Some countries may be inefficient, and raise trade barriers. This will damage the industries of other countries, who will in turn raise further trade barriers and perhaps cause the system to collapse.

The world is becoming more international in its outlook, as suggested by concern about issues such as Third World Debt. In order to try to increase their manufacturing capacity and increase their liviing standards to western levels, some Third World countries have borrowed from western commercial banks. In order to repay their debts, certain of these countries are now destroying their rainforests. The loss of this ecosystem is affecting sea levels, climate, and the very air that we breathe the world over.

In such circumstances it perhaps seems old fashioned to be too selfish about international trade, regarding it as something we can use in order to benefit ourselves at another country's expense. We should realise that we live in a world community and find ways of trading which benefit all countries while conserving our natural resources.

Acknowledgements

The New World Encyclopedia, Bay Books 1982.
Economics Textbooks — various.
EEC — information leaflets.
ELAC Ltd. — publicity material.

Special thanks to the management of ELAC Ltd., the office in Adare Street, Bridgend, of the Member of the European Parliament for South Wales, the staff of Bridgend County Library, and the people who answered my questionnaire. Other details were gleaned from the Business Sections of various newspapers and the BBC2 "Money Programme".

GENERAL EXAMINER COMMENT

The methodology of this assignment is very good indeed. It moves from the particular to the general, from the local to the national, from the known to the unknown. We like the way in which Ken began by setting himself "tasks". This is a good way of beginning to think about the issues involved in an assignment. If you can set yourself a series of related tasks, you can then draw up a timetable so that you can complete these tasks according to a schedule. This will help you to cope with the pressures of producing coursework for several subjects.

We think there is clear evidence that Ken has *learned* and *matured* while undertaking this assignment. This is a fascinating possibility – the idea that coursework not only *tests* candidates, but also enables them to *learn* and leaves them better educated *after* the test. If this is true then it is a strong argument for coursework over conventional examinations.

Some of Ken's earlier work is rather clumsy; the surveys at the beginning of the assignment were a very good idea, and an excellent way of getting busy, collecting facts and figures relevant to the topic. However, the notes and explanations surrounding the surveys are not very well written or properly thought out. Yet, by the time Ken begins to deal with the EEC the quality of work is improving, until he reaches his conclusions which are excellent, and his final analysis of Britain's current position is quite impressive.

Most students embark on their GCSE courses at the age of about 14, and complete them when they are 16. Parents are only too painfully aware that their young ones grow up very quickly at around that time, and teachers also often notice an improvement in the quality of work (examiners refer to this as "maturation").

Several times in this book we have recommended that you make an early start on your coursework, and we feel that this is *essential* in order to stop yourself becoming overloaded as the final deadlines loom ever closer. On the other hand, if you write an assignment *very* early on in your Fourth Year, it might be worth re-reading it, if possible, before final submission. You will almost certainly not have time for a complete re-write (this would anyway defeat the whole object of starting early), but you might be able to insert one or two additional paragraphs or some further conclusions in the light of experience which you have subsequently gained.

We will use the NEA marking scheme to assess this assignment. Ken scores highly on the first two "Levels of Response", but we have not felt able to award such a high proportion of the marks available for the third. We feel that he could have linked the assignment a bit more closely to economic principles, in particular the principle of Comparative Advantage which which is very important to international trade. Although this principle is mentioned at points in the assignment, we feel that it is not successfully linked to the topics which Ken discusses. For this reason, Ken has achieved the first of his two aims rather more successfully than the second: he has answered the question he set himself, but has not really tested the hypothesis.

Recognise, select and present relevant data: 12 (out of 15). Analyse and interpret the data and apply it in an appropriate wasy: 13 (out of 15). Make reasoned judgements based on economic principles: 5 (out of 10). Total: 30 (out of 40) = 75%.

FINAL NOTE

The examples in this chapter, and the model answers in Chapter 3, offer you quite a bit of guidance. You might find it a useful exercise to make a list of general 'do's' and 'don'ts' so that your work achieves the best, and avoids the worst, of the points illustrated in these examples.

Understand the assessment objectives, develop your skills, and coursework will be something that you can take in your stride. The techniques you develop here, and the knowledge you gain, will also be valuable in your written papers and help you to achieve a good overall grade in GCSE Economics.

Above all, remember that coursework is not something to be afraid of; producing a good assignment is hard work, but it is worthwhile and it can also be a great pleasure. So, get started; good luck; and . . .

ENJOY your Economics coursework!